AUDACIOUS*AF*

AN EMPOWERING GUIDE TO RUNNING AN AUTHENTIC BUSINESS

Amanda King

GFB

GIRL FRIDAY BOOKS

 GIRL FRIDAY BOOKS

Published by Girl Friday Books™, Seattle
www.girlfridaybooks.com

Produced by Girl Friday Productions

Design: Paul Barrett
Production editorial: Jaye Whitney Debber
Project management: Reshma Kooner

Image credits: cover © Shutterstock/El Nariz

ISBN (paperback): 978-1-954854-78-9
ISBN (e-book): 978-1-954854-84-0

Library of Congress Control Number: 2022915487

First edition

This book is dedicated to my nieces and nephews.

*Aaliyah, Danny, Emma, Maddie, Mikey,
Ricky, and Sophie, this book is for you.*

*May you always allow your lights to shine
as bright as possible in this world.*

*May you live your life as authentically
as humanly possible.*

*May you dream so big and so wild that it scares the
shit out of everyone who dares to question it.*

*May you always trust yourself, be selfish,
and experience so much joy in your life that
you can barely contain your smiles.*

*My life became better every single
time one of you was born.*

*I love you more than I can put into words. Thank
you for bringing so much joy and love into my life.*

CONTENTS

INTRODUCTION

My heart begins to pound as I lift my phone. I slowly press the Bank of America button and feel the panic take over as the app begins to load. You are freaking out over nothing, *I silently say to myself.* It's not as bad as you think it is. Take a deep breath. *But the app opens, and I see my bank account balance staring back at me and realize how truly wrong I was. I have every right to panic, because glaring back at me is a negative number. I knew that my financial situation wasn't the most ideal, but I had no idea how bad it had truly gotten. Now the negative balance burns a hole in the back of my head, revealing to me exactly what I have been trying to avoid recognizing: that I have failed. I spent the entire year of 2018 doing what my coach told me to: hungrily copying and pasting every strategy she handed over to me, mimicking her every move, and investing all my money into courses. And now I have fuck all to show for it. No profitable business, no clients, nothing but a negative account balance and a year's worth of feeling frustrated as shit.*

But it wasn't for lack of trying.

My coach, a mentor I had invested in to help me create structure and implement strategy in my coaching business, was a brilliant business strategist, meaning she helped online entrepreneurs build systems (workflows, email marketing campaigns, Facebook ad management, sales funnels) in their businesses to make efficient sales. She was a multi-six-figure coach, and she was crushing it; her strategy was bulletproof.

She had sat on Zoom with me for hours helping me build my website, create and run Facebook ads, and structure my offers and service packages. She had talked me through the exact strategies she used to grow her successful business, and I had eaten it up. I had spent months at the computer, replicating everything she taught me, hours crafting my product suite on Kajabi (a platform for hosting online courses), and days working on my graphics in Canva to make sure they were beautiful, eye catching, fucking perfect. I had also spent weeks building my website to showcase who I was to the world, all while building my business from scratch. I had been doing everything right—all the things the online entrepreneurial world tells you to do.

"Niche down!"

"Build a website to sell your services!"

"Get branding photos and create graphics that are aesthetically pleasing!"

"Run Facebook ads to bring in new clients!"

You name it, I did it, and happily I might add, because all I wanted to do was succeed; all I wanted was to create a business that could support me financially and give me the freedom I was craving. I would have done anything to achieve that goal, even if it felt wrong to me, overwhelming, and overcomplicated. I was willing to do it all to reach the success I desired.

I had already spent an entire decade working in corporate America, having to abide by their rules and structures, always having someone telling me what to do. My last corporate America job was as a pastry chef for a local Washington, DC, restaurant chain. Along with a massive culinary team, I was opening their newest location in Mount Vernon Square, and the opening turned out to be a disaster. The owners had spent way too much on staffing before the restaurant opened and therefore decided to rush the opening to attempt to recoup some of their money. This meant that the entire opening staff worked nonstop from August to December, fourteen-hour-plus days, seven days a week, in absolute chaos. When the time came, the launch was disorganized—and worse yet, the owners refused to listen to the culinary team's recommendations. One of the owners' brilliant ideas had been to introduce a program featuring twelve flavors of doughnuts for one dollar each. I had warned them it was severely underpriced, with food and labor costs alone estimated at five times the amount being charged, but they didn't care. Flash forward to sales of one thousand doughnuts a day, with me working from 6 a.m. until 11 p.m. just to keep up with the demand. No surprise: I became completely burned out. I wasn't sleeping, was living off eggnog lattes, and felt like I was going to crack at any second every minute of the day.

And then, on New Year's Eve in 2017, I did fucking crack. One of the owners, just coming back from vacation, was pissed off that I didn't have enough doughnut flavors up and ready for brunch that day. He proceeded to berate me in front of the entire kitchen staff over and over again.

"Do you not fucking care about your job, Amanda?"

The 6' 5", balding, heavyset manager towered over me, screaming while I tried to pull a bread pudding from the oven.

"You need more fucking doughnut flavors up there!"

"I am trying," I said. "I have eight out of twelve up there. The rest are coming."

"They need to be up there right fucking now! What is your problem today? Do you want to keep your fucking job?"

I felt the breakdown coming. I placed the bread pudding on the cooling rack, turned my back on him (as he was continuing to scream at me at the top of his lungs), and walked to the exit door that led to a small stairwell. He proceeded to follow me until I walked through the door and slammed it in his face. I broke down in that stairwell for over a half hour: sobbing, dry-heaving, shaking so hard I couldn't stand, so I sank to my knees and just broke. I walked out that day with no prospects and no plan; I just knew I couldn't do it anymore. I couldn't work in the culinary industry one more day, and I also couldn't work for people who didn't listen to me, respect me, and take me seriously. I desired freedom. I wanted to be my own boss, and I would do anything to not go back to corporate America. Happy Fucking New Year.

So I went into 2018 looking for a fresh start, and I hired a coach who was an expert in business. Her strategy had worked for her, so it had to work for me, right? But it didn't. Not because it wasn't brilliant—it was—but because it didn't feel right for *me*. I was compromising what *I* wanted for my business, how *I* wanted to show up and run it. I was giving in to what my coach and other entrepreneurs were peddling, and that was why a negative bank balance displayed on my phone at the end of the year. I had sacrificed what I wanted to do for what were supposed to be the "right" business moves.

Throughout the year, I never spoke up to my coach and said, "I would like to try something different," or "This doesn't work for me; can we brainstorm another way?" I ignored my gut, and my intuition, and when I finally saw that negative bank balance and felt frustration and even a lack of passion, I really had no one to blame except myself. It was a bitter pill to swallow in a moment where I already felt defeated, like a failure—when I wanted to throw in the towel and never look back. But it was the moment of epiphany that I truly needed.

What if I'd had the audacity to do shit differently? What if I gave myself this next year to run my business the way I wanted, the way I desired? What if I showed up in the online space as 100 percent authentically me? What's the worst that could happen? I was already fucking broke and had already tried all the things that had been recommended. So what if I just gave myself the permission to run my business in a way that felt right to me, without all the overcomplicated strategies?

That negative dollar amount on that day in December 2018 was the catalyst that caused me to finally say "fuck it" to running a business that had started to feel inauthentic to me. The next year—2019—was going to be different. It was time to have the audacity to show up in a completely different way. To run my business from a place of alignment, doing only the things that really felt fucking good to me, and not just because I felt that I *should* do them that way. I didn't know it then, but that moment would become the foundation of the Fierce as F*ck brand—a business dedicated to coaching women on how to own their authenticity in an oversaturated online space—and grow it into a multi-six-figure operation in just eleven months. All organically—no Facebook ads, no sales pages, no website, no email marketing—none of the strategies that the online industry tells you that you "need" to grow a successful business. Just me.

That was my strategy: having the audacity to do what feels good and being unapologetic as fuck about it. And it's still my strategy, one that's allowed me to grow Fierce as F*ck to earn a multi-six-figure paycheck annually.

I'm guessing, if you've picked up this book, that maybe this sounds familiar. Ask yourself: Are you also running your business into the ground doing what others tell you to do? Even though it doesn't feel right, are you pushing through because you believe you're willing to do whatever it might take to create success for yourself? Even if it's starting to feel icky, gross, or just plain wrong, are you still doing it all, implementing all those countless strategies taught in the online entrepreneurial space but still not getting the results you want—that you fucking deserve?

If you're feeling as frustrated as I was, you have every right to be. If you feel like you're two seconds from quitting, returning to corporate America, and giving up your dreams, then you're in the right place. Because I am inviting you to give your business one more chance, to give *yourself* one more chance, to do things differently this time. I am asking you to take a leap of faith, to believe in yourself, and in me, and allow me to help you achieve what you desire and deserve from your business.

But we need to get a few things clear before we jump off. Is this a business book that will help you reach success in your online business regardless of what services or products you sell? Absolutely, 1,000 percent, that is our goal here. *But* if you think this is a book that is going to jam down your throat "business strategy" in the traditional sense (build a website, create sales pages, the five-step process for creating a profitable framework, how to manage your Facebook ads), you should turn back right now, because that isn't what you are going to get from me.

What will you receive then? What is my promise to you? My promise to you is that, by the end of this book, you will have the tools to run your business from a place of alignment, a place of self-trust, so that you can create a business that fuels your soul and your bank account.

I spent a decade in corporate America being shoved into a box that I desperately wanted to break out of; that was the whole reason I decided to step into the online space. Yet, my first year in the online realm was spent shoving *myself* back into the same box, just in a different space. My expertise lies in going from not being able to sell a fifty-dollar dessert course in 2018 to selling out a twenty-thousand-dollar mastermind, a yearlong virtual business container that provides coaching to entrepreneurs, in 2019. *That* is the power of showing up in your business the way you want to, in full fucking alignment.

Now, obviously there was strategy involved during this

process, but it wasn't something overly complicated or full of funnels or Facebook ads. It was simplistic. So simplistic, in fact, that other online entrepreneurs thought I was straight-up crazy for doing it. They thought it wouldn't generate the revenue I needed to be deemed successful. And yet this simplistic strategy was exactly what did work.

Are you ready for it? OK, grab a pen and paper so you can write down all the deets: I showed up on Facebook Live every single day for an entire year. That's it. I mean, obviously there was a little bit more to it, but really? Not much. I showed up. I coached. I helped. I sold. Does this mean you can put this book down right now, duplicate my strategy, and find massive success in your business? Possibly, but that is not what we are doing here in this book; we are not just copying and pasting a strategy that works for one person into another person's business. My business strategy worked for me because it *felt good to me*. I've seen past clients try to implement this exact strategy and not reach the success they desire, because it isn't about the strategy. *It's about you.*

What I am doing in this book is teaching you how to create your business from a place of authenticity, meaning it's 100 percent representative of who you are as a business owner, a leader, a human. I am here to show you how to make aligned decisions—decisions that feel good on a soul level, so that whatever happens in your business you can trust yourself to come to the right conclusion that benefits you the most. I want you to have the audacity—the nerve, the guts, the grit—to say "fuck it" to what doesn't feel right. That is what I am here to do today.

There you have it, the secret sauce for running a successful business: audacity.

Audacity is about the way you show up in your business. Audacity is what worked for me in 2019 after that negative bank balance, and it was what helped me get to a place where business became effortless, where everything just flowed. Yes, it was easy—easier than the sixteen-hour shifts I used to pull as a pastry chef opening various restaurants. Easier than surviving the Florida heat in August dressed in a Winnie the Pooh costume and trying not to pass out as I greeted children. Easier than the last day I spent in corporate America, crying hysterically in the stairwell of the restaurant where the owner had just screamed at me for not having enough doughnut flavors available for brunch, after I'd worked for almost three months straight without a day off. So much easier than all of that shit. Through audacity, my business responded to my natural abilities to be outspoken, to create communities, and to empower others to create action in their lives, all of which made it feel as effortless as inhaling. It became something I didn't have to *try* to do; it was something I just did.

Audacity was what helped me step into my true power. The reason my business exploded and my life changed wasn't simply because I created the most revolutionary business strategy known to man. It exploded because I also had the fucking audacity to

- Live authentically even though people would hate it
- Be bold, be vulnerable, be polarizing
- Take up fucking space in this world
- Take no shit from anyone
- Be unapologetic AF about who I was
- Be loud, swear, and demonstrate my passion
- Challenge the status quo, the right and wrong way to do things
- Break the wall of the box and light that bitch on fire so that I couldn't be put back inside it by anyone, even myself

Audacity can create a ripple effect across the entire planet.

Having the audacity to be yourself is the most powerful thing you can experience in your entire life. It's real, it's bright, it's bold. And it's also a power that can change the world. By embracing my own audacity, I created a massive ripple effect that, in addition to helping me succeed in my own business, gave others in my industry—the underdogs and outcasts who felt they couldn't fit into the box that everyone was trying to stuff them into—the opportunity to finally feel seen and heard. I was able to give a voice to the people who felt they couldn't show up as themselves but instead had to appear as some grounded Zen yogi person who had all their shit together. I had the audacity to be vulnerable, to share my fuckups with the world, to feel safe being passionate and polarizing—and that shook people. When someone chooses to have the audacity to be themselves unapologetically, it allows every person around them to do the same, granting permission and revealing possibilities of what their lives could be. Audacity can create a ripple effect across the entire planet.

Every time you step into your audacity, your confidence will grow and you'll become stronger. Doesn't that sound like what you want to be? I want that for you. But for you to embrace your audacity, you need to be able to say "fuck it" to how other people want you to run your business. A "fuck it" moment is a time in your life where you say, "Fuck it, fuck everyone," and you have the audacity to trust yourself, trust your decisions, trust that you know the answers for your business better than anyone else, that you have what it takes to make it in the online space.

In this book, I am sharing with you thirteen moments in my life and business when I have had the audacity to say, "fuck it." Each of those "fuck it" moments has been a catalyst for success in my business, which is what I want for you, too. My hope is that, by reading about my personal experiences, you can become more confident, trusting yourself to scream "FUCK IT" from the rooftops and following your own intuition to build your own authentic business. Every chapter also contains attainable action steps to move you closer to the business you desire, as fast as humanly possible.

What if you had the audacity to show up in the online space as the true, authentic AF you? Imagine what might happen if you allow yourself these "fuck it" moments:

> *Fuck it to what everyone else is telling you to do.*
> *Fuck it to how everyone else is running their business.*
> *Fuck it to allowing others to dictate how you show up in your business.*
> *Fuck it to the frustration you feel building up in your soul.*
> *Fuck it to spending hours working on a goddamn graphic.*

We have all been told throughout our lives—by our families, our friends, and society—to be a certain way. You must look a certain way, behave a certain way, speak a certain way. And let's all be real: it's fucking exhausting—am I wrong? It is exhausting to spend your entire life living inside this box that everyone and their mother is trying to shove you into.

And you don't need to anymore. Audacity allows you to tell the world to fuck off and to live your life the way you want, as your truest, most authentic self, without the thousands of masks you have worn over the years, as someone who no longer needs to appear as everyone else's representation of who you are. It takes a certain level of confidence to bank right when the rest of the world shifts left. It takes a certain amount of backbone to allow yourself to live an authentic life when the rest of the world is trying to have you fall in line like the little toy soldier they want you to be.

Look back at your business. Are you currently just sitting on the sidelines, stuffing yourself back into that pretty little box because it makes you feel safe, comfortable? Or are you allowing the world to see the true you? The messy, fucked-up, wrong, brilliant, powerful, bold, daring you?

Whichever your answer, at least we know where to start. The first step to fixing a problem is admitting to yourself that there is one, and that *you* are the one who caused it. Oy, just knocked the wind out of you right there, didn't I? It's OK—this is the most powerful part of your journey. This is step one and the first "fuck it" moment right here:

Fuck it: Recognize that you are the problem. But take comfort in knowing that you are also the solution.

I know the idea of saying "fuck it" to people and things that you've grown comfortable with, including yourself, can be a mindfuck and is probably causing your stomach to flip and bile to rise in your throat. And that's OK. This won't always be an easy journey, but it will be a journey worth taking. And remember: all this isn't going to happen at once. This isn't something that will one day just—*poof!*—happen. It's an accumulation of a bunch of moments over a span of time, so take them one at a time. There is no reward here for finishing first or saying "fuck it" the fastest; that is not how this journey works. Every "fuck it" moment needs to be celebrated, and each time you stand in your confidence and say this, it will become easier to do the next time. My hope is that, by the end of this book, you won't be as scared to say "fuck it"; in fact, you will be able to say it so quickly that it will feel as easy as breathing. My goal is to have you embracing your own "fuck it" moments in your life, owning the ones you've already had, and creating some new ones. By sharing my personal journey with you, with my own stories of fuck-ups, obstacles, and ups and downs, I will help you realize that you are not alone in this venture; we are doing this together.

Because you know what? You have that power inside you. You have the ability to create massive change in this world, create a ripple effect, and build a business that leaves a legacy. The difference between those who are successful in the online business world and those who aren't comes down to whether they choose to access and harness that power. The decision is completely up to them, and now it is completely up to you. What will you choose?

Are you ready? Let's go show some fucking audacity.

CHAPTER ONE

———

F*CK IT: SAY NO!

It's now the end of 2019 and I have my first online meeting with my new one-on-one coach. She is a brilliant business strategist who is the queen of creating operating systems in business. Basically, she helps create workflows, sales funnels, effective email marketing campaigns, ways to repurpose content on multiple platforms, and so on. One of the aspects of her business that attracted me to her was that she has a tool for everything, and I, someone who has quite literally built my business by the seat of my pants, now want to start putting systems in place to help me scale more efficiently.

At one point during the two hours together, she asks me, "What is your five-year plan for your business?"

I just stare at her like a guppy, wide eyed, opening and closing my mouth slowly. "Ugh, I don't know."

"Well, where do you see yourself? Do you want to just teach group coaching programs?"

By this time, I have been selling out multiple group coaching programs with every launch. These programs vary in duration (four weeks, three weeks, five days, etc.) and focus on different aspects of running a business. "Badass Bitch Academy" focuses on launching your business organically in thirty days using social media as a sales funnel. "Be a Boss Bitch" is about simplified organization skills you can add to your business without getting overwhelmed. "From Fear to Fierce" is a mindset program teaching entrepreneurs how to step out of fear and into launching their online business. I also have a few one-on-one clients who are entrepreneurs looking for more hands-on support to launch their businesses. I run every single one of my programs live, meaning I show up on videos a few times a week and teach my clients while answering whatever questions come up. I devote so much time to every single program, which involves a lot of energy, effort, and showing up on my part.

"I mean, I want to write a book, do public speaking events, host some in-person retreats, a large summit—stuff like that?"

"OK, great," she says. "How do you expect to do all of this while still running your group coaching programs live all the time?"

"Uh . . ."

"You can't be in two places at once. And you don't want to be hosting events and having to jump on live video calls at the end of the events to run your courses, do you?"

"No . . ."

"Well then, it's time we start looking at how to make your group coaching programs more passive."

And her point was completely valid. She knew I had big dreams and visions for my brand, and she also recognized that the amount of time I was spending to show up in all these courses was taking away from the time I would need to pursue other avenues in my business.

But my entire fucking business had been built on running my courses live, and I truly loved it. Everything about being in the moment with my people, connecting with them, being there to answer all their questions when needed, the relationships I was creating—all of it felt so freakin' aligned. I didn't want to give that up. So I just stared back at her in that first meeting, feeling like I had been punched in the chest and trying to hold back the tears. I couldn't even speak. The idea of letting go of my live courses made my soul scream, *"WHAT THE ACTUAL FUCK?"*

And then she said the most brilliant thing to me:

"Listen, if what I am saying to you isn't aligned with you, if it doesn't feel right, you can say no. I need you to tell me no. Because if you don't tell me that it doesn't feel right, then I can't find something that is right for you."

Say no? Wait, what? I could say . . . no? Such a simple concept, and yet so baffling. I was paying her for her expertise but was allowed to say, "Nah, man, that doesn't work"? That couldn't be right. She made more money than me. She knew more than me. Clearly, I needed to do all the things she said I should do. But she argued that this was my business, and I was the one who got to make the rules. She was just there to offer perspective and support.

Mind fucking blown.

I want to clarify that this isn't about not taking your mentor's or coach's advice, because their advice *is* great. It's what you pay them for. What this is about is having the *audacity* to speak up and say "no" when things aren't aligned with you. If your coach says something along the lines of "I believe you should create a twelve-step email marketing campaign to nurture your audience, build trust, and convert them into members of the group coaching program you are launching in the spring," and you absolute fucking detest writing emails, don't be afraid to speak up and say, "Hey, I really hate emails, and that strategy doesn't feel good to me. Can we adjust it or think of something else to do together?"

Look, I know I'm about to take you on a journey of learning to say "yes" to creating the business that you want, but the

What this is about is having the audacity to speak up and say "no" when things aren't aligned with you.

first step is learning to say "no." It's not about not being open and coachable. It's about learning how to trust your instincts so you don't end up letting all the external noise drown out your own voice.

Hear me out: Obviously there are times when we need a coach or advisor of some kind, where we do need help with strategy. It would be all sorts of fucked up to tell you that you don't need a business coach, as I *am* a business coach and I truly believe that, with the right mentor, you can achieve greatness. If you decide to work with a coach, they can provide clarity for your business because they can see what you aren't seeing when you are so thick in the shit that you are missing what is right in front of you. And there are times when your coach's strategy will really resonate with you, and if that is the case, then, my God, go forward with it and implement that strategy immediately. Don't second-guess it. *If it feels good, it is the right decision.*

But sometimes, that's not the case. There are times when we are tempted to take every single word uttered by experts and coaches as gospel, even when their strategies just feel off. When you take someone else's words over your own gut instinct, shit can get messed up. If you end up following a strategy that isn't aligned with your values or desires, that doesn't feel good, it won't work out. I know, that was a bitch smack right to the face, but that is my style, tough love. You need to recognize that no matter how incredible the strategy might be, if you have massive resistance toward it (not feeling like you want to show up that way, avoiding doing said task because it doesn't excite you, or making excuses about why you can't do what is required of you), you won't implement it properly. Your energy won't be behind it. And when it comes to your strategy, you need to be excited by it. You need to want to implement it. You need to be energetic about it, even if it is a little throw-up-in-your-mouth scary.

So this isn't about telling your mentor and her strategy to politely fuck off. It's about having the confidence to say, "Fuck it. I get to build my business the way I want, not the way everyone else is building theirs." Why? Because this is how we build businesses from a place of authenticity, from a place that feels right inside our souls. There isn't a cookie-cutter strategy that works for all of us; if there were, we'd all be millionaires. I know you can spend all day looking at coaches on Instagram who have become successful because of their strategy, but it's *their* strategy. It works not because of what it consists of, but because the energy behind it is authentic and has been right for them every single step of the way. If you don't have the audacity to say no to your coach, and you build your business based on their strategies, it will feel wrong every step of the way. It will feel icky and gross, and you will begin to resent everything about your business, because at this point, it really isn't *your* business.

So go ahead and learn their strategy. It's important, and there's stuff that people can teach you that will save you time and heartache. *But* check in with yourself about how it aligns with you. Be honest: Is it a no because it's going to make you a bit uncomfortable, or is it a *HELL NO* because it goes against your values?

TAKE F*CKING ACTION
BUILD AN ALIGNED BIZ

Step 1: Weed out the dead weight. Go through your current business strategy, if you have one, and ask yourself, *What do I absolutely hate about this strategy? What feels yucky? What part do I avoid the most? Where do I feel the resistance coming up?* It's time to toss all that aside. Give yourself permission to let go of the parts that don't serve you. (If you don't have a defined strategy yet, go directly to step 2.)

Step 2: Have the audacity to say no. The next time your coach—or anyone else—tries to give you strategy advice that doesn't fit, say to them, "Hey, listen, that's great advice, but it doesn't really sit well with me. I don't think that is the right move, but I would love to explore some other options or perspectives with you." It's OK to say no.

Step 3: Put your energy into the strategy that turns you on. A lot of times, when we are trying out many different strategies, our energies are split up 6,432 different ways. Imagine if you could focus all that energy on something you actually love to do. Yes, it's possible. And yes, it can be easy. Identify which aspects of your strategy are really exciting, and focus your time there. If there are aspects of your strategy that are necessary, but you hate doing them, hire someone to do them for you.

Step 4: Always check in with yourself. No matter where you are in your entrepreneurial journey, there will be times when you will lean toward allowing others to making decisions for you or trying someone else's strategy or method. That's OK; you should allow yourself the freedom to play with different modalities. But always, always, always check in with yourself. If things are starting to feel icky again, trust your instincts and allow yourself to release whatever that is. So what if you've already paid for it? You believed you needed it in the moment, and now it no longer serves you. Let it go.

TAKEAWAY: For your business to thrive, you need to have the audacity to say, "Fuck it. This is the business I created, and I get to run it the way I want to, not how everyone else says I should." The first step in saying *yes* to creating your dream business is learning how to trust your instincts and build your confidence in knowing when to say *no*. It's such a freeing feeling when you fully embrace it.

CHAPTER TWO

F*CK IT: SHOW YOUR FACE

I take a deep breath as I walk through the automatic doors of the CVS, mustering up the courage to achieve what I need to. The aisle 4 sign instantly beckons me to it. I walk down the aisle, glancing left and right, hoping that no one can see me. I mean, who wants to be seen near the diet foods and products? The Atkins diet snack bars pass my line of vision, and next come the South Beach ones, and then the SlimFast shakes. What I am looking for is nestled in with the rest of the diet pills: a bright-yellow box shining in the distance, with red lettering that catches my eye. The irony that this box shares these same bright colors with America's number-one fast food chain isn't lost on me, and I wonder whether it is a marketing ploy or an accident. Who knows? I lock the box in my vision and quickly make my way to it.

Dexatrim. I need it, and I need it now. I grab the box and quickly slip it into my pocket before anyone can notice. My heart begins to palpitate, and my mouth quickly fills with saliva. The nausea hits me hard. My nerves tingle. But I know this is the hardest part. I'm almost there. I start my journey back down the aisle, as I've done many times before. I can do it again. Not wanting to look suspicious, I walk down the beverage aisle next, glancing at the variety of sodas in front of me. Decisions, decisions. I grab the Diet Pepsi, steadying my hands as they begin to shake from the adrenaline coursing through my veins. I quicken my stride and make my way to the cash register, where I set the soda on the conveyor belt.

The gentleman smiles at me. "Just the Diet Pepsi today, Miss?"

I smile back and nod. Yes. I need him to just check me out so I can be done with the charade. He looks at me and states the amount, which I clumsily pull out of my pocket, dropping the change onto the counter loudly. I wince at the sound.

"Sorry," I say, while the voice in my head echoes, You've done this before, King, you've got this.

I am thirteen years old.

I didn't want to have to steal diet pills when I was a young girl; it didn't make me feel good, and I sure as hell wasn't doing it for the adrenaline rush. I *hated* going into the store month after month to steal, but because I was underage, I couldn't *buy* them, and I knew my mom wouldn't approve, so this was my only option. I had been taking Dexatrim for months at this point, and I was dropping weight like crazy. In a matter of about two months I had probably lost around fifteen pounds.

And people noticed. They complimented me, said how great I looked, and commented that I must be "growing out of my baby weight." They attributed my weight loss to being a kid during summer and getting additional exercise. My family, and even my dad, praised me for how great I looked, and the boys started to notice me, too. I started feeling confident for the first time in my entire life. I was also finally able to shop at the Deb—a clothing store for teenage girls that specialized in smaller sizes—with the rest of the girls. My life was looking up, and the acceptance I was getting from everyone was addictive.

But I was also already having side effects from the pills. I mean, there was enough caffeine in them to put down a damn horse. My heart rate would beat so fast sometimes that I thought my chest was going to explode, but eventually it would always calm down, so I justified the discomfort as a sacrifice for weight loss. The appetite suppressant in the pills was incredible; I couldn't even eat a full McDonald's cheeseburger from a Happy Meal without feeling stuffed. And no one knew. I hid the pills in my closet under all my clothes, and I would sneak into the closet in the morning with some water, take the pill, and go on my merry way. It was my dirty secret, but unlike secrets that lead to heartbreak and lies, my secret was leading to attention and praise, to finally feeling noticed and worthy. So every day I took that little pill with a smile on my face, not giving two shits about the side effects. Mind you, this was before 2004, when ephedra, the second-greatest ingredient in Dexatrim, was banned from all diet pills.

Knowing that this pill could potentially kill me didn't matter because, at thirteen, who cares about having a stroke? That is for old people. At thirteen, all that matters is that you are accepted and you belong. All that matters is attention and boys. After tipping the scales at 120 pounds when I was just eleven years old, and having the school nurse say, "Oh now, that is too much weight," I had built up a complex and believed that, to be happy and loved, I had to be thin. This story was reinforced in my head when I started to lose weight and everyone started to treat me differently. They no longer asked me, "Are you sure you want to eat that?" They no longer watched in judgment as I ate a cookie. The girls at school stopped hurling the word "fat" at me whenever we would get into arguments. Life was fucking good, and there was no way in hell I was going to let that go. It meant too much to me at this point, so if I had to break the law to achieve happiness and love, I was going to do it.

Needless to say, dealing with my weight and body image

has been an uphill battle my entire life. Year after year, I punished myself for not looking the way I wanted to. With one fad diet after another, my weight yo-yoed during my later teenage years and then well into adulthood as I repeated the same cycles over and over again. There were many years when I could maintain my weight, but even that wasn't good enough. Always. Had. To. Be. Thinner. Once in a while, I would become happy with my body and start to see myself making progress, but then a picture from an unflattering angle would appear and send me down the spiral of shame because I could never be thin enough. All the progress I made wouldn't mean jack shit because it was never enough. *I was never enough.*

I know I am not alone. Lots of people, and especially women, struggle with how they look. A lot of self-help gurus, when discussing body image, will tell you there is a time when you must love and accept yourself. That you must love your body to love yourself as a whole. Well, I don't necessarily agree with this statement. Hear me out: I don't know if I will ever truly *love* my body. I do believe it is beautiful and strong, but to say that I accept it as is, that I will never focus on the flaws, would be a lie. Even the gurus who preach "love your body" have days when they have just come off a cheesecake-and-ice-cream bender and feel heavy and bloated.

So I am not going to sit here and tell you to do something if I have not fully embraced the idea or notion myself. But what I will tell you is that I've learned to say "fuck it" despite what all the gurus preach. Fuck it: *I don't have to love my body. But I do have to respect it.* Even if you never come to terms with the way your body looks, you can recognize that your body is a part of you, and it deserves some respect. Your body has given you life; your body has given you strength; your body has endured years of beating and battering. It deserves some motherfucking respect for what it has been put through. You do not have to worship it, but you do have to respect it so you can learn to really focus on all the beauty that is inside you, that *is* you.

Do you ever go to the gym, and while you are sitting in the locker room, a woman, probably in her early seventies, walks by you stark naked, while the twenty-to-forty-year-olds are trying to strip underneath a towel so no one can see their bodies? Well, that beautiful seventy-year-old woman has no more fucks to give; she has full body acceptance and that is how she does it. She has hidden herself for decades, and as she has reached her "senior" years, she has come to a realization that she deserves the right to look however the fuck she wants to look. She has finally disrobed (figuratively and literally), and she is at peace. She is happy, even if it took her decades to reach this point in her life.

Our challenge is to figure out how to be at peace with ourselves in the online world. Let's be real here: the internet is a brutal-ass place, and even if you are a grown adult, it can make you feel like a small child on a playground. People will not hesitate to showcase all your flaws and push you to the limits. You will have people jump on a live video just to say you're ugly and have random men DMing you that "you'd be prettier if you'd lose ten pounds." There are no limits to what random-ass people will do to make you feel like shit and sabotage your business. I'm not telling you this to scare you; I am telling you this so you'll understand that it's not easy for anyone—even someone extremely secure in their body—to allow themselves to be seen in the online space.

Most of the clients I work with are women, and their biggest fear when it comes to being seen—especially online—is how others will judge them for the way they look. They often flat-out don't feel comfortable enough with their bodies to appear on live videos or even to take photos of themselves. In fact, some of my clients actively hate their bodies. If they can't even look at themselves in the mirror, how can they show up with authentic energy in a space that is notorious for ripping people apart for just existing? It is much easier, and feels better, for them to sit behind their computers, hide behind pretty infographics, and build their behind-the-scenes shit rather than showing up as the faces of the brands. Trust me, I get it. I have struggled with my body image my entire life, feeling like I was never pretty enough, never attractive enough, never able to live up to society's expectations. It was hard to learn to be the face of my brand when my struggle to accept my body has been a part of my natural being.

But we cannot occupy our rightful space in the online world if we are struggling with how we take up physical space in our lives. We need to allow ourselves to be *seen* in both worlds if we want to be successful. You have to say, "Fuck it, I may not love my body, but that's OK. I don't need to love it, but I do need to respect it." You need to have the audacity to respect your body where it is right now, and to become comfortable with it and able to own it in the online space. You need to show up and be seen.

Because when you do, you will shut up every motherfucker out there who needs to put their two cents in. You will jump-start your motivation and feel more empowered to keep on showing up in your most authentic form. And you will inspire others to do the same. And you know what that leads to? Making fucking money. Why? Because you are empowering your audience, through your actions, to *take action*. You are causing them to *move* by creating a bond with them because you were able to do something that others weren't: give them permission to respect themselves. And that is the most powerful thing you can do for people—inspire and empower them to create change. In other words, *your* self-respect changes people by creating impact, and that impact in turn builds brand loyalty and generates income.

You need to show up and be seen. Because when you do, you will shut up every motherfucker out there who needs to put their two cents in.

Look at it this way: when you allow your body to hold you back from showing up in your business, you are leaving money on the table. Your audience, your followers, are looking to connect with you—all of you, not just your words or your voice, but your face and maybe even your entire self. They want to see you in the same way they want to be seen *by* you. When you allow your insecurities to take priority over your audience, and you hide from them, you prevent them from getting to know you. You prevent them from being able to trust you, and you can't expect them to buy from you if they have no idea who you are, can you? Trust leads to sales, and without sales, you will not achieve the dream you desire. Also, when you are able to step into your power, respect your body, show up, and allow yourself to actually be seen in the online space, you give permission for everyone else to do the same.

TAKE F*CKING ACTION
RESPECT THE SHIT OUT OF YOUR BODY

Step 1: Respect your body. It has gotten you here. It is strong. And it drives you forward, which drives your business forward. If you cannot respect your body, you will not allow yourself to be fully seen in the online space, and you cannot create a business without being fully seen. Think of all your body has gotten you through, think about all it has survived. It's a goddamn machine—a powerhouse—and it deserves some damn respect. Jot down the answers to these questions if you are a fan of journaling, or ask yourself these prompts and talk them through out loud:

1. What is some of the shit your body has been through?

2. How did your body survive?

3. How does your body contribute to your survival every single day?

4. How can you start respecting your body more today? What are some ways you can be more positive toward your body?

Step 2: Pour love into your body. I am dead-ass serious about this, so don't roll your eyes at me. Look in the mirror and say one positive comment about your body each day. Start small if you need to, with something like "I have pretty eyes," and then work your way up to bigger things. Focus on those aspects of your body that make you feel strong, nurtured, safe. Tell yourself what a magnificent beast you are every day to show your body the respect it deserves.

On days when I am really struggling, I look at myself and say, "What would I say to my niece if she were standing right here?" I wouldn't let her shit on herself, so why should I allow myself to do that? I will act as if my niece is talking shit about herself and needs my help to see her true beauty. I will turn that energy inward.

Step 3: Show ya face! This step may take some time, so start small with this one, too. Can you post a picture of yourself today, put up a fifteen-second Instagram story, or maybe go balls to the wall and jump on a live video? How else can you start taking small steps every day to allow yourself to be seen in your business? Remember, when your audience can see you, they can connect with you on a deeper level. Graphics and sales pages can't form that level of connection; only *you* can.

TAKEAWAY: Your body is strong, your body is beautiful, your body is power, *you* are power. A massive part of business is showing up and being *seen*, so it's time to get comfortable in your own skin. You can't make the impact on the world you want to make if you keep hiding.

CHAPTER THREE

F*CK IT: F*CK THE HATERS

One Friday while growing my Fierce as F*ck brand, I decide to try to kill two birds with one stone by livestreaming my Free Coaching Friday program on both TikTok and Instagram at the same time. This program, which has become a massive hit, allows me to interact with my community live. I answer their questions about business strategy, mindset struggles, Human Design, etc. I give them free advice and tell them how I do things, such as how I convert people from my free five-day program (and from this weekly event) into new customers. I am completely in my element, and all this interaction is feeling amazing. Until about ten to fifteen minutes in on this particular day, when I notice the TikTok comments start rolling in.

"God, put some makeup on, you look like shit."

"Man, do you see her mustache? Look at it shining in the light."

"Her mustache? Look at her fat-ass thighs."

"You mean fat ass in general, lol."

"Thunder thighs!!!"

And they keep on rolling in. Although my Instagram

audience is unaware of what is going on because I am using two
separate phones and they can't see the comments, my TikTok
audience can see every negative thing posted, which fuels even
more people to post more negative comments.

"Shut the fuck up, no one cares about what you have to say."
"She is fucking annoying. Shut up, bitch!"
And holy freakin' shit, does it start getting to me. The com-
ments pop up on my screen one right after another, relentlessly,
as these random-ass strangers continue to rip me apart. I start
to get thrown off my game completely. I begin to stutter. I also
get paranoid about the "mustache" comments; even though I
know I don't have one, I keep trying to hide the top of my lip
from the camera. All the while, I am trying to answer the legiti-
mate questions, but my hands start shaking and I lose my train
of thought. I feel like I am back in high school, with everyone
pointing and laughing at the fatty trying to speak on stage. My
heart pounds so loudly I can hear it.

I was not prepared for this brutality. I had known about
Facebook's trolls, but they paled in comparison to those wolves
lurking in the dark corners of TikTok. For a moment, I thought
I was going to be sick right in front of everyone. I had never
ended a live video early in my entire career—not for deliveries
at the door, dogs throwing up, or others interrupting me—but
that day I almost did because this shit shook my ass to the very
core. I kept thinking, *Shut it down, King! Shut it down!* And I
almost did.

But then I remembered something: these people know absolutely nothing about me, and they are sitting here trashing
my appearance. What a sad-ass life they must live if the high-
light of their day is getting onto some random person's live
video—mine in this case—and trashing them. Fortunately,
I was able to have the presence of mind to ask myself why I
should let some sad sack ruin the work I was there to do because they were jealous of my ability. *Awwww, hellllllll no,* I

thought. *Fuck it, fuck the haters!* My work was too damn important to be shut down by some shallow comments from trolls. I summoned the audacity to not give a fuck about what those people thought. I was there for the people who needed to hear my message that day—the ones who needed help stepping into their power—and they were there live, too. They were watching, and in fact I gained more than twenty followers just from that one live video.

At that point in my career, I had become a pro at showing up on live videos. From January 20, 2019, to January 20, 2020, I had gone live every single day. It was how I built my audience, my brand, my identity. My audience looked up to me as *the* live video expert at that point in my career, and I had dealt like a pro with haters and trolls jumping on my live videos just to start shit so often that it no longer fazed me. At first, of course, it hurt, but the more it happened, and the more I recognized that their hatred had nothing to do with *me*, the easier it became. So, as an expert on live video, I naturally had thought I was ready to tackle the newest social media platform that was hot and popping at the moment: TikTok. I was nervous, but I had been posting prerecorded videos on that platform for about a year and figured it couldn't be that bad. Famous last freakin' words.

Since then I have received many rude, mean, hateful comments criticizing the volume of my voice, my language, and the pace of my presentations, in addition to the comments about how I look. A lot of entrepreneurs know that this negativity can come with being seen in the online space, but it is still a difficult situation to deal with when you meet it head-on. It's easy to say that you will be fine, that it won't affect you, but to see it right in front of your face? That is a whole different beast to slay. Why? Because deep down inside of us, we all have a need to be liked. And when you face the world in the online space, people will not always like you.

People will be unkind, brutal, or uncaring—sometimes for quite literally no reason whatsoever. Your very existence might even irk them to the core. But if you want to show up authentically in the online space, you need to know what lies ahead for you: the good, the bad, and the downright ugly—and the World Wide Web can contain the ugliest of them all. That's why you have to just say "fuck the haters" and do *you*. You have to have the audacity to not give a shit about what strangers think about how you look, the tone or volume of your voice, the way you stand in your truth. Because the fact of the matter is this: you cannot be liked by everyone in the online space; it will never happen. People will dislike you just to dislike you, without rhyme or reason. They just will, and if you go around caring so much about their words or opinions, you will soon begin to dull your light and lose your authenticity. You will start showing up for *them* and not for *your people*. You will start trying to people-please to make everyone happy, and in doing that, you will lose not only yourself but also your audience—and then, once again, you will lose your income stream. You need to get over this notion that you will be liked by everyone, because that is just not possible.

And you need to remember this: it's not really about you. The hurtful comments they spit out at you, the mean things they say—although they sound personal, they're not really about *you*. I know, that is hard to believe because they will come at you with the rage and fury of a beast and try to tear you apart, limb from limb. And how can that not be personal?

The irony is that these people who attack you really have very little power; you are the one who holds the power. You can hold up a giant mirror to them and show them just how little they have. They are the ones without confidence or true courage. They are the ones who are vulnerable. You can show them who they really are, and they won't be able to handle that shit.

Bullying and negativity are a power struggle; it's a way someone can try to assert dominance over you, which is what these people are trying to do. They don't feel dominant in their lives, so they assert their dominance over unsuspecting victims on the internet. But when you stand up to the haters, you own your power, stripping them of the power that they believe they have over you. And nothing gets to a hater more than losing *more* of their power. The challenge is to not let them drag you down but instead to remain strong, speak your truth, and stand in your beliefs.

TAKE F*CKING ACTION
DEAL WITH THE HATERS

So what the hell do you do in these situations, when haters and trolls are talking trash about your content or your live videos?

Step 1: Remember that your message fucking matters. When you see the negative comments come in, you may feel overwhelmed as fuck. One, this is completely normal, and two, that's when you need to take a second to remember that you aren't here for them; you are here for *your people.* You have to remember that your message is too fucking important to let some asshats cause you to stop speaking. Remember, there is someone out there really needing to hear your opinions, beliefs, and perspectives on that day, and if you let the haters control your time, attention, or words, your audience will not get to hear your message. Take a deep breath, slow your heartbeat down, and visualize the person who needs to hear you.

Step 2: Block the haters. The great thing about live videos is that you can ask a friend or one of your teammates to monitor the comments on your videos. I wish I would have known this before jumping on my first TikTok LIVE. Let a friend know you are going live and let them block all the haters that jump on and start talking shit. It's OK to block people who are just there to be mean and hurtful. You owe them nothing. The faster you get them out of your feed, the better. Ask a friend or bring an iPad with you if no one is available. Then find the hater and hit that block button ASAP.

Step 3: Keep on going. I know: in that moment when shit hits the fan, you may feel like crawling into a hole and shutting down your account, your post, and your livestream. But I am begging you not to. When you shut your content down, you allow the haters to win. You give them the power. And if you do that, do you know what will happen? They will keep on coming back into your life and starting shit over and over again. Why? Because they have nothing better to do. But when you keep on going, you retain the power. You show them you are unafraid, that you cannot be bullied. Moreover, your audience will see you standing in your power against the haters. They will see how powerful you are, and they will want to emulate that. They will show up despite the trolls, and *you* allowed them to do that. So whatever you do, do not stop. Don't let the haters win.

You cannot please everyone, and when these haters do show up—and they will—it means you are doing something right.

TAKEAWAY: The online space can be a scary place when it comes to dealing with complete strangers who attack you for no reason whatsoever. You cannot please everyone, and when these haters do show up—and they will—it means you are doing something *right*. Yes, you read that correctly: right. It means you are being polarizing and vulnerable, and you are speaking your truth, and that is fucking incredible. So when the haters show up, keep your focus on the people who need to hear your message and realize it's the Universe's way of saying, "Keep on going, bitch!"

CHAPTER FOUR

———

F*CK IT: LET GO OF SUPPORT

I have been on a fucking roll in this live video, spitting fire with every single word that leaves my mouth. I am in my element, and my audience is eating it all up. This is fire! Preach! This is resonating so hard right now! The positive vibes are flowing on my live video until a little bubble pops up from my dad's Facebook account.

The second his picture appears, I cringe because I know exactly what is going to happen as soon as I end the video. I instantly think, Tone down your language, *and of course I do, but it feels inauthentic. I try to shake it off and end the video as powerfully as I can even though I know a series of texts will soon be waiting for me on my phone:*

"You really need to stop talking like that on Facebook" and "I get you are trying to do something good, but you should choose a different way to say it" and "I like what message you are saying, I just don't like how you are saying it."

This happens after every single live video. And fuck, it drives me absolutely crazy. Here I am, trying to get his support while trying to help make a positive impact on this world, and all he cares about is the fact that I say fuck *a few times. It finally comes to a head after I receive about the one hundredth text message from him about my language and how unbecoming it is.*

"If you don't like what I am saying," I text back, "and if you don't think you can support it, then block me." And good God do I mean it. I have spent my entire life trying to be the image of what he wants me to be, and it is about goddamn time that I get to live my life the way I want. Now, I have finally mustered up the audacity to see that I don't need him to be on board and to believe I can do this shit. I don't need him cheering me on. And it is the most freeing moment of my life.

"Listen here, Missy," he replies. Missy *is his pet name for me when he is mad. "Maybe I will block you."*

"Great," I retort. "The block button is located on my profile. Go hit it."

My journey, I now see, is no longer about his support of my work. It's about what I want, and right now I want to say fuckity fuck fuck *as many fucking times as I damn well fucking please.*

One of the biggest reasons entrepreneurs really struggle in their first year in business is that they are expecting everyone in their lives (family, friends, etc.) to support their decisions to enter the online space and break free from the confines of corporate America. In fact, their need for support often starts to outweigh their need to just do the fucking work, and all the underlying emotion winds up derailing them when they start to feel resistance. They start weighing every single business decision against what their moms will think, what their dads will say, or what Becky from the PTA will see. It becomes a constant uphill internal battle, which inevitably leads to frustration, resentment, hurt, and anger, and eventually they either completely give up or start watering themselves down in the online space to appease everyone else.

When I decided to start my own online business, it definitely took me some time to be able to handle haters and internet trolls, but for the most part I was well equipped to handle the negative feedback that came my way—except for the feedback from my family.

I wouldn't say that my family was entirely *un*supportive, but the support they did offer came with what I like to call conditions. And this was especially true for my dad. He and I had always been close, and I grew up trying to become a version of myself that would gain his approval. As I started my personal development journey, and truly began to find myself, I wanted him to be happy with the woman I was becoming. Instead, our relationship became strained. I felt that he just didn't understand "how to handle" me, my personality, and my belief system, and the more I found myself and my voice, the more he would push back. He is more conservative than me, believing that a woman has very specific roles in life: to be a wife, to take care of her husband, and to breed lots of babies that *she* is supposed to raise and take care of. He believes that women are meant to be dainty, pretty, angelic creatures who float on clouds of 1950s misogyny and smile through it all. Women are also supposed to look a certain way, be a certain weight, and act a certain way, and he would back up his sayings with "Well, my generation believes . . ." or "Your generation [insert insult here]."

When I started in the online space, he wasn't against me owning my own business or being a coach; he was against the way I was showing up on social media—in particular, the language I used. He doesn't like when women curse. "It's unladylike," he often said. My brother was allowed to say anything he wanted to, with as much colorful language as possible, and my dad wouldn't bat an eye. But because I have a vagina, I was not given that same right. I remember one time when I yelled the word *vagina* at him, and the look on his face was that of

You have every power within you to accomplish everything your heart desires, and you do not need anyone else to support you to achieve that. You need to support yourself, and that is it.

someone who had just eaten an entire pack of Warheads candies at once: pinched, shocked, and instantly regretting their decision. That image will forever be burned into my mind.

You can imagine then how much he loved his only daughter showing up on social media, dropping one f-bomb after another, saying the word *cunt* on a live video, and using *bitch* in all the titles of her courses. But this was *my* business, not his, and I was going to run it the way *I* wanted to, whether or not he could accept it.

Y'all, you do not *need* the support of your loved ones to create an online business. You may *want* their support, but you have every power within you to accomplish everything your heart desires, and you do not need anyone else to support you to achieve that. You need to support yourself, and that is it.

I know you may be reading this right now and thinking to yourself, *But what about my significant other? I can't possibly continue this business without their support.* But before you even wonder, let me say that you most certainly can. I have worked with dozens of women who do not have any family support when they start their businesses, and it doesn't hold them back from achieving their dreams. Yes, it presents some bumps in the road; yes, they have to set up some clear-ass energetic boundaries with the family. But lack of support doesn't completely halt their business growth or keep them from being successful. What matters most is that you feel safe, both in a physical sense and in terms of your nervous system. As long as your safety is taken care of, you can set your own boundaries about what is necessary for you to thrive in your business.

The best thing about having an online business is that you are introduced into a community that not a lot of people understand: a community of misfits. This community is labeled "crazy," "risky," "too bold," and "unconventional" by the outside world. Some people just don't understand why the hell someone would want to own their own business. Other people don't relate to the draw of online entrepreneurship. But although this community is seen as the land of misfits by the rest of the world, you get to make friends with people who know exactly what you are going through, who understand who you are, and that is what makes it so fucking special. Brené Brown said in her 2019 Netflix special, *The Call to Courage*, that we should stop giving a shit about the spectators outside the arena, because they will never understand us; instead, we should care about the people who are getting bloodied, beaten, and bruised *inside* the arena with us. *They* are your people. And it is so fucking true. So use *them*—the people who are hammering away at their computers every day, selling on social media, and experiencing what you are experiencing—as your support system. Don't bother with the people who are sitting on the outside saying, "Da fuck?"

TAKE F*CKING ACTION
LET GO OF THE SPECTATORS

Step 1: Be your own fucking captain of your own ship. The captain has a crew that she surrounds herself with, a crew that she can trust. The crew helps hoist the sails, set the anchor, and support the captain with whatever she needs from them. The crew assists the captain in navigating obstacles, passing storms, and overcoming whatever else comes their way. They help make sure everyone on the ship arrives at their destination safely.

What the fuck does this have to do with business? As an entrepreneur, you also need to surround yourself with a crew that supports you, that has your back 100 percent of the time in your business. Your crew needs to challenge you, of course, but they need to be people who know your vision and are willing to help you arrive at that vision safely.

Step 2: Leave the others at the dock. Do not allow people who do not support you, and your move into the online space, onto your ship. And, most importantly, *do not force them onto your ship!* Let this lot wait on the dock until you get back home. Why? Because if you allow them on your ship, they will constantly question your decisions, your motives, and your moves. In so doing, they will both make you question yourself every step of the way and drive you further away from yourself. If your energy is put into battling them every second instead of keeping your eyes on the ship's path, you will inevitably wind up with a shipwreck.

Step 3: Set them boundaries. Before you conclude that your business and life with your family or spouse cannot coexist, recognize that having both is possible but only if you set some strong-ass boundaries. What do these boundaries look like? Maybe you don't discuss your business with your family but instead reserve that topic for those who do support you. Maybe you come right out and say, "I don't care if you support me in this, but I will not have you shitting on me." Or maybe you let them know it's OK if they don't support you, but they do have to respect you. Whatever boundaries you need to set, set them, and set them firmly.

TAKEAWAY: You need to stop thinking that you need support from your family and friends. The support you need is from the people who show up and need you. And the funny thing that often happens once you start gaining success is that all those people who wouldn't initially support you will start to admire and envy you, and before you know it, the bitches will be jumping into tiny-ass rowboats, paddling their little asses off, to get onto your ship. But even then, you'll need to remember that you don't need their support and never did. You only needed yourself.

CHAPTER FIVE

F*CK IT: PUSH AGAINST THE GRAIN

"You are running your business completely wrong," she says, staring at me, her eyes feeling like daggers into my fucking soul. "No, you will be shut down for doing that. You can't be running your business like that. That is so irresponsible of you to do that." She just keeps hammering into me.

It is March 2020, literally the week COVID-19 hits the United States, and I am attending a mastermind in San Diego, California. It is my second year in business, and I have invested in a yearlong business mastermind that includes three in-person meetups. This is the first (and will end up being the only) meetup of the year, and I've been unbelievably excited to meet the other six women who are able to attend the event as well. When I arrive at this event I am also coming off the high of my business exploding in 2019, and now I really want to use 2020 as a time to focus on adding more structure to my business, hiring team members to support me, developing training and onboarding procedures for new clients, etc. I don't want to just replicate my results of 2019; I want to double them. So here

I am, in the living room of an Airbnb overlooking the San Diego skyline, ridiculously excited to gain as much knowledge as possible over these three days.

My coach, who is extremely well connected with other high-earning coaches in the industry, has set up guest speakers and panels to come to this event and teach us all about their tricks of the trade. When I heard that this particular woman was coming, I was full of glee. I had been watching her videos online for about a year, and I'm not going to lie, I was completely fangirling out. As a seven-figure earner in the industry, she is the queen of utilizing live video in my eyes. I had wanted to learn ALLLLLL the tricks she was going to put out there. Like a schoolkid, I'd gotten out my notebook and had my pen in hand, ready to take all the notes from the teacher's lecture. But now it's all fallen apart as she bombards me with critical questions.

"Why would you think that would be OK to do?

"You know Facebook can mark you as spam content and take down your entire profile?

"That isn't the right way to run your business, you are causing yourself a lot of trouble."

She continues to berate me in front of the other women, whose eyes dart back and forth between the expert and me. My head keeps screaming, Defend yourself! Speak up! She has no idea about who you are or what you do. AMANDA!!! FUCKING TALK! *But instead I sit there completely dumbfounded and, for the first time in a really long time, fucking speechless. The room feels like it's closing in on me, and the energy in the room shifts as tension rises. My face grows red and my blood begins to boil; I clench my jaw so hard that my teeth hurt. But still not a fucking word comes out of my mouth.*

This whole debacle happened because one of the other women in attendance brought up the fact that I was running my online coaching business from my personal Facebook page instead of my business page, which at the time wasn't something that coaches were doing. The traditional "rule" was to run all your business marketing from a Facebook business page because Facebook ads from your content had to come from your business page. But since I had no intention of running Facebook ads, and the visibility of Facebook business pages among Facebook users was dropping drastically, I chose to run my business a different way and use my personal page to promote my coaching services.

In case you're not immersed in the online coaching culture, there has been and probably always will be a debate about where you should market your services using social media. Therefore, when this particular coach heard that I was on the opposite side of the fence, she handed my ass to me on a silver platter with all the Thanksgiving trimmings, accusing me of being irresponsible, not doing adequate research, and essentially, not being very smart.

I could feel everyone's eyes on me in that moment, and I did everything within my power not to cry, but fuck, man, did it hurt. It was like someone had stabbed me in the gut, turned the knife, and now was just watching as I bled out slowly and painfully. One of the women in the room even tried redirecting this coach's attention by chiming in, but it didn't help. It felt like time slowed down or like I was watching a movie in slow motion, and I was brought back to adolescence: the time the teacher catches you not paying attention and calls your name. You jump, startled, and think to yourself, *Oh, fuck.* The entire classroom's eyes are fixed on you, and the teacher, with an annoyed look on his face, is waiting for you to answer, and meanwhile you have no idea what the fuck is going on. You feel the color rush to your face, your cheeks grow warm, and you sit there humiliated in a moment that feels like it lasts forever. Now there I was, a grown-ass adult feeling that exact same humiliation and pain, and yet this time, I had done nothing wrong that day or in my business. I just hadn't done things *her way*, and that irked her.

Eventually, after she had drawn and quartered me in front of the room, she went back to her normal lecture, acting as if she had done nothing wrong. Honestly, I believed she realized she had overstepped a little because, for the rest of the lecture, she refused to make eye contact with me. Every time her eyes would almost meet mine, she would dart them across the room. I just sat there, like a quiet little girl, waiting for it to be over. Waiting for feeling to come back to my body. Waiting for a second when I could get up and go cry.

And although, at the time, I wished I could speak up, I eventually realized I didn't *need* to speak up in the moment. I didn't *need* to defend myself or my actions. Why? Because I didn't do anything wrong. Just because she couldn't wrap her head around the way I ran my business, and just because I ran my business differently from how she ran hers, it didn't mean I was wrong for doing so. It meant I had a different and unique perspective on things, and some people can't handle shit being different from their own. Or they can't handle an idea that doesn't conform to their ideas. Or when others decide to push against the grain. I realized I needed to say, "Fuck the grain."

I needed to have the audacity to own my pushing against it and to let go of how she tried to make me feel bad about being different. That's shit. It's for the birds. The online space is full of amazing, unique perspectives, and you know what businesses stand the test of time? That are the most successful and most talked about? The ones whose CEOs decide to have the audacity to go against the grain. When Oprah went from a daytime talk show host to creating OWN, her TV network, she went against the grain. When Whitney Wolfe Herd, while working for Tinder, realized there should be a dating app where women initiate the contact, she went against the grain and created Bumble. Going against the grain takes courage because it is so drastically different from what the world expects from you, but it is also the very thing that sets you apart from the rest of the world.

The coach at that mastermind had no idea who I was, and she failed to even find out by asking questions, which was on her. One of the core values of a coach should be to never assume you know someone else's journey or reasoning, but instead to have an unbiased opinion. If you want to know more, to get further clarification, you should ask questions. She broke the cardinal rule of coaching when she assumed she knew everything about my business and judged me without allowing me to clarify why I had decided to do things differently.

But more importantly, I triggered her. The fact that she lashed out so vehemently when she learned that I went against what she believed, the way she thought, and the way she felt—and that I was successful in my business—obviously means that it struck her pretty hard. But isn't that exactly why we are on this planet: To represent alternative perspectives and to show that there isn't just one path to the finish line? To demonstrate that the world is full of different avenues to get there? To acknowledge that there is a whole world beyond the box we are currently residing in? Isn't that the beauty of interacting with people from all different walks of life? Isn't that why we don't all look, speak, and act the same? Being unique is absolutely fucking terrifying, but there is so much beauty that lies inside this way of being. Forging your own path, allowing yourself to be the way you want, and having the courage to run things the way you choose is how you obtain the life you have always wanted. It is how you make sure your soul is aligned, what turns you on and gives you the crotch tingles.

The biggest fear that comes into play when we consider forging our own paths and being the first person to do

Forging your own path, allowing yourself to be the way you want, and having the courage to run things the way you choose is how you obtain the life you have always wanted.

something a new way is that there is absolutely no guarantee it will work out. There is no—and never will be any—amount of certainty that comes from the experience. No one who has forged their own path has known for a fact that it was going to work out in the end. They had faith, and they had hope, but they also knew that it might be an absolute fucking disaster. And they did it anyway. However, let me challenge you and ask you this: Is following the path that others have laid out for you giving you guaranteed results? No? Is it giving you the life and business you desire? No? Aren't you reading this book because things aren't working out as well as you wished they would? Yes? Then wouldn't it be fucking fun, even though there may not be any certainty in going against the grain, to see what shit would happen when you do?

Don't just believe me; let's talk about Jen Sincero, the author of the massively popular personal development book series You Are a Badass. I had the privilege of meeting her in DC while she was on a book tour, and she served as an example for me when it came to going against the grain. You Are a Badass gained notoriety because, at the time her books were first being published, they were so vastly different from every "love and light" self-help book out there. They went completely against the grain of the personal development world, and because of that, they exploded, ultimately selling five million copies worldwide and taking her from being broke as fuck to a seven-figure author. That is the raw power of going against the grain.

TAKE F*CKING ACTION
FORGE YOUR OWN PATH

Step 1: Reflect! Think about where you're holding yourself back. Where are you allowing other people's thoughts and feelings to dictate how you show up in your life or your business? What are you so afraid of? *Who* are you so afraid of? For example, are you thinking of becoming a women's sexuality coach, but you were brought up in a conservative household and are terrified of what people in your community might say? Explore these questions, dive fucking deep, and figure out what is keeping you from deciding to say, *Fuck it, I will forge my own path.*

Step 2: Accept and embrace uncertainty. Remember, life is never going to be certain, so why not *play* with the idea of uncertainty? Rather than looking at every single thing that could go wrong with forging your own path, think about what could go right. What possibilities lie ahead of you? How can the potential of these possibilities completely change your life for the better? Going against the grain is deeply uncomfortable because it's easier to do what everyone else is doing.

Step 3: Dismantle your current beliefs. Everyone has told you that you "have" to do things their way, and somewhere along the line, you began to believe them. You allowed their limitations, their beliefs, to become your own, saturating your skin and sinking into your bones. It happens to the best of us. But we need to dismantle these beliefs brick by brick because they aren't necessarily the only way. And they aren't necessarily the right way. They are ways that worked for *some* people, but that doesn't mean they will work for all people. It's time to sort through your belief system: Did you create the belief that your life had to look a certain way or was it another person's bullshit that was pressed onto you? If it's truly your belief, keep it, but if it's someone else's bullshit, it's time to toss it, literally. Write the belief on a piece of paper, crumple it up, and throw it in the trash—or better yet, light that shit on fire. Watch that belief burn before you, releasing all the limitations it has put on you and your success.

Step 4: When everyone goes right, go left. Forging your own path means defying what everyone else is doing and doing the opposite, challenging the status quo. In 2018, I was told I had to run my business a certain way (needing to invest in Facebook ads, having a website, needing to create landing pages to sell my services), and it all felt wrong. But that is what everyone at the time was doing, and they were having success with it even though I was not. The next year, I decided to forge my own path and dismantle my own beliefs that things needed to look and be a certain way to succeed. I dismissed conventional wisdom that said investing in Facebook ads was the only way to find potential clients, or that relying on a twelve-page sales spread would sell my program better than presenting it live, or that having a website was the only way to make my business "real." I defied the social norm, and because I did what I wanted to do rather than what everyone said I should do, my business exploded. Never, ever be afraid to step away from the pack and create your own path in another direction.

TAKEAWAY: The path you are creating is *yours* and only yours. There will be people along the way who will question your every move and tell you what route to take; go ahead and let them. But realize that just because their path is easier, it doesn't mean it's the best one. And more importantly, this isn't about them. Forging your own path is about creating a life or business that sets *your* soul on fire. That means being willing to do things differently, pushing against the grain, and responding to the naysayers with "You just watch me, bitch."

CHAPTER SIX

———

F*CK IT: ACKNOWLEDGE YOUR WORTH

As I wrap up a live video on Facebook, I share the details of my Badass Bitch Academy with my audience and tell them they can direct-message (DM) me with any questions. Immediately a DM pops up in my inbox with a question about the price. I know that when someone starts a conversation off with "How much is it?" they are already walking into the sale hesitant. Therefore, I typically try to ease them into conversation first and get to know them a little better (building the connection/ trust factor) before I dive into pricing.

"Hey! Thanks so much for reaching out after my video! I'd love to help you. What about Badass Bitch Academy makes it feel like a good fit for you?"

"I want to launch my business," the potential client says. And again she asks about the price.

"The program is $400, and I can offer a six-month payment plan of $67 if that is something you'd be interested in! What type of online business are you wanting to launch? A coaching business? Product-based business?"

"$400? You can't be serious."

I hadn't been sure what to charge, and when I reached out to my mentors to ask their advice on pricing guidelines, a majority of them responded with "Charge what feels right." But my confidence was pretty nonexistent when it came to selling at this point in my career, and with this being my very first course, I didn't want to overprice it. So I decided to offer this as a beta run, which allows you to give your course a test run for some paying customers but at a discount. That way, if anything goes wrong (which it always does), they don't feel cheated or swindled, and you get to work out the kinks of your course before you charge a higher price. It's a win-win situation for both parties. Having already invested about fifteen thousand dollars into different masterminds and courses, I know what online business courses focusing on launch strategy typically charge: from seven hundred to as high as three thousand or more. I decided to charge four hundred with a super affordable payment option.

But this type of situation is also when online entrepreneurs become triggered—and rightfully so. You are pouring your heart and soul into your course, your product, and your service, and someone is now questioning your value, your worth. This is the time in the sales conversation where there often comes a fork in the road, and you need to choose a path.

Path 1: *You instantly think,* She is right; I am out of my depth, and this is priced way too high. I need to decrease the price, *which leads to online entrepreneurs cutting their prices ridiculously low because they can't see their own value.*

Path 2: *You take a deep breath and trust that you priced your offer at the right amount, that just because this* one *person is questioning your value doesn't mean everyone will. That even though this* one *person doesn't see your value, it doesn't matter, because* you *see your value. This path is you sticking to your prices and being able to handle objections when they come your way.*

I choose path 2.

"Yes, I am serious," I reply. "It's an extremely well-priced course. I am also offering super affordable payment plans. You can do a six-month one for $67 each, if you'd like."

"That is absolutely ridiculous."

"What is?" I ask.

"That you are charging $400 for a business course. There is no way it is worth that much."

"Actually, I have invested in business courses that are almost triple that price and had less value. This course will help you get your online business up and running in 30 days in a way that is simple, efficient, and fun."

"You are out of your mind then," she says. "I would never pay that amount of money for a course."

I knew deep in my soul what my course was worth, and I had dug deep into my pockets to offer ridiculously affordable payment plans to try to help as many people as possible. And yet, some people still weren't happy. Even now, I know that no matter what I charge, whether it's one hundred dollars for a masterclass or twenty thousand for a mastermind, there will always be someone who questions my prices and, therefore, my worth. What that early conversation taught me was that I needed to say, "Fuck it, I deserve to be paid for my work," and I decided to have the audacity to know my value and to be unapologetic as fuck about it.

So many of my clients want to create a massive impact on this world, or at least they want to create financial freedom for themselves and their families. But to make money in your business, you have to be willing to sell your offers out there in the world. And to sell your offers, you have to put a price on them. And this is where so many entrepreneurs get caught up in the online space: not recognizing their value and worth and charging accordingly.

"But shouldn't I give it away for free first," they ask, "just to get some testimonials?" Or they say something like "I just don't know what to charge; everything feels so icky." My own accountant once said to me, "I have no idea how you can charge twenty thousand dollars for a mastermind. I could never do that!"

There is so much guilt wrapped around money, and the desire to have more of it by charging other people for our work, and yet the number-one reason many of us start our businesses is financial freedom. How does that make any sense? There is absolutely nothing wrong with wanting more wealth, even if you have a good life already. I do not care if you are poor as fuck or the wealthiest SOB in the country; every single person deserves financial freedom. And to get there, you have to charge for your offerings.

Moreover, if you cannot see your value and own your worth, how do you expect the Universe (or God, Spirit, Source, whoever you speak to) to bring you the clients you desire? If you cannot see your value, no one else will be able to see your value.

Imagine this: your toilet in your house becomes clogged and water is spewing all over your bathroom floor. You know you can't fix this problem yourself; you know this goes beyond your capabilities. So you immediately call a plumber to come help you. The plumber comes into your house, unclogs your toilet, cleans up your floors, and completely fixes your problem. When the plumber hands you the bill, do you ever for one second stop and think, *This person doesn't deserve to be paid for their work*? Absolutely freakin' not! You run to your wallet, and you pay that person for their work because they deserve it. And then you go on to refer your friends to the person who saved your day. Their work is valuable to you, is it not? How much value comes from not having shit overflowing through your house?

You are the plumber of people's lives. Whether you come

in to plunge their hearts and clean up their tears or you offer a product that simply makes them happy, you are making their lives better, and your work will be noticed. You *deserve* to be paid.

TAKE F*CKING ACTION
RECOGNIZE YOUR VALUE

To charge your worth, you need to recognize what a fucking badass you are.

Step 1: Identify your badass qualities. Let's start at the beginning: How do you help those around you? Let's get clear on the transformation you provide people. How are your clients when they first come to you? What do they need, and how do you help them with their transformation? Grab a pen or marker and a giant Post-it and write down all the ways you help the people around you. Write down all the badass qualities you have and why people would be lucky to work with you. Once you write them down, hang them somewhere in your office where you can look at them every single day. This way, when you start to question your self-worth and value, you can look at what a fucking badass you are. You can recognize your value. When you recognize your value first, others will recognize it as well.

Step 2: Pick your pricing. Stop listening to coaches and other mentors, and figure out what price *you* are most confident charging. What price can you say without feeling butterflies and nervousness? What price can you quote while keeping eye contact with someone and not flinching? What price do you know deep in your soul is the right price for you? When

You
deserve
to be
paid!

you figure out an aligned price—one that leaves little room for argument—you will be able to close your sale because you will have the confidence to charge what you need to charge.

Step 3: Practice, practice, practice. Now that you see your value and have established the price that feels aligned with your soul, start practicing your sales pitch. Get in front of a mirror and do it for yourself. Practice on friends and family. The more confident you become, especially with saying the price, the easier selling will become. Any time you are starting to feel self-doubt, go back and look at the visual representation of your badassery from step 1 and scream out loud, *"I AM ONE VALUABLE MOTHERFUCKER!"* Keep practicing, and before you know it, your confidence in selling—and in handling any objections—will grow.

TAKEAWAY: You put your heart and soul into your work. You help change people's lives and create transformation. That shit isn't easy, and that shit has value. To be successful, my dear, you've gotta see your value and be unapologetic as fuck about it.

CHAPTER SEVEN

F*CK IT: TRUST YOUR DAMN SELF

"All in all, your expenses for business growth were a bit high. You spent forty thousand dollars this year," my accountant says. We are meeting to discuss year-end results, and *"business growth"* is her term for the amount of money I had been investing in group coaching programs, masterminds, and one-on-one coaching. *"Which is why your profit margins are down a bit more."*

I almost throw the fuck up. Forty thousand freaking dollars? Are you kidding me? *Little do I know, it is about to get so much worse.*

Now, for you to understand how I spent such a massive amount of money in one year on coaching, I need to talk a bit about the beginning of 2020. That was the second year in my business, and everything had been trending toward another extremely profitable year. So I came into 2020 with high expectations, not ready for the shit show that was about to ensue.

As it turned out, 2020 was a rough year globally. In fact, I almost named this book *2020: The Year of Shit Sandwiches* because much of it revolves around the most trying, hardest, and saddest year for me and for the freakin' world. I had been extremely blessed to have had a wildly successful year in business in 2019, defying the odds of the coaching world once I learned to go firmly against the grain. I was polarizing as fuck, and unbelievably happy and secure in myself. It was so magical that I believed I could do and achieve anything.

But then between the pandemic, the speed of my success, and everyone telling me to slow down, I freaked the fuck out. It was like I hit this level of success and happiness and thought, *OH SHIT! Things cannot be this good; something bad is going to happen. The rug is going to be pulled out from under my feet. What if I wake up and this business is gone tomorrow?* I slammed on the brakes and began to worry that my success wasn't safe or sustainable.

Like it did for most people, the COVID-19 pandemic whipped me—emotionally, physically, and financially. Income started to decline rapidly, due to people losing their jobs or having to support their families during shutdowns. Some clients dropped out of programs, unable to afford the monthly payments. Some stopped buying altogether. And with this rapid decline in income, I began to think that my business, which I had poured my blood, sweat, and tears into, was going to close the doors before we even had a chance to truly begin.

The amount of pure emotion that ran through my body from March 2020 through the rest of the year was terrifying. My anxiety shot through the roof, which caused me to get into my head every second of every day, and without being able to spend time with friends and family, I spent the entire year secluded and spiraling downward. My mental health tanked. I completely and utterly lost my sense of self.

I share this with you because your journey to activating your power and stepping into your true self won't always be easy, and sometimes you will lose your way. It happens; we are human, and we make mistakes and fail. But we don't really learn from those mistakes unless we talk about them. Unless we allow people to see our ugly, vulnerable sides.

A personal journey is not linear. Not even fucking close. It is full of ups and downs, and sometimes you can make it to the top of the hill and see all your potential, only to then fall back down the hill. The journey is messy, but it is also human and beautiful. Hopefully my story of falling so far down that hill, in the midst of a pandemic and with revenue sinking, will help you realize you are not alone.

Feeling completely disconnected from myself, I thought if I had a little guidance from a coach, they could give me the answers I needed to find myself again. But my extremist ass didn't just sign up with one coach. I signed up with a coach for spiritual guidance to help me reach my higher self, a coach to certify me in Human Design (a personality trait modality similar to the enneagram model that uses a combination of quantum physics, astrology, kabbala, and the chakra system), a coach for business strategy, and a coach to teach me how to become a better coach. I also received three separate certifications in Human Design: Fundamentals, Business, and Manifestation; these would help me teach my clients how to find themselves again. Of course, I was hoping that somewhere along the way I'd also find *myself* again and get some answers to why nothing felt right anymore and why I was so scared and unbelievably lost.

When my accountant alerted me to how much I'd spent on all that, I was shocked. I knew it was a lot, but damn, I didn't expect it to be that high. To make matters worse, she also discovered that I had been inadvertently failing to make some payments for those programs since the previous July, even though my card had been on file and I'd signed up for automatic payments. Those added up to another fifteen thousand dollars in "business growth" expenses for 2020.

I completely lost my shit. A complete and utter break-down. I literally burst into tears, and God bless her, she tried to help me breathe and get ahold of myself in the moment. To believe that I had spent forty thousand dollars was nauseating, but to realize that I had *actually* spent fifty-five thousand was *DEVASTATING.* I had the money, but I was triggered by the fact that fifty-five thousand fucking dollars would have been enough to pay off my car twice! Enough to put a deposit on a sick house! Enough to pay the salary of an employee for a year! I had spent all that money to find the answers to all my problems—the solutions I thought I needed—and you know what that taught me? Both the problem and the solution to my problems was:

ME.

Yup, I had spent a complete year looking outside myself, grasping at straws, and spending an obscene amount of money to realize that I, Amanda motherfucking King, had all the an-swers to my problems inside me. I was fucking pissed. Not at the coaches or my accountant, but at myself for spending all that money to find outside validation, to "fix" me, and to find the right path. And I hadn't needed to.

But that experience taught me the most valuable lesson that I will now carry with me for the rest of my life: fuck lis-tening to everyone else. I have always known, and will always know, the right answers. My intuition will never be wrong, and no one knows me better than I do. I knew this shit. I knew that listening to your intuition was deeply important; I mean, I made it a main theme of chapter one of this damn book. But somewhere along the way I'd forgotten. Forgotten my own most important rule. No one else will be able to provide the answers to my solutions. Only I can. And I would need to have the audacity to actually trust myself.

What does this story have to do with you? It's time for you, too, to stop searching outside yourself for the answers that you desire. It's time to stop purchasing the courses because you believe they hold all the answers to your problems. It's time to stop believing that everyone else is the key to your success and happiness and start recognizing it's fucking *you*. I know, you may be thinking this is easier said than done, because, my God, it really is. It is so much easier to throw money at a problem, to purchase a course that will be *the* course, to look around and have everyone else figure shit out for you. It is so much easier, but will it be the most beneficial? Absolutely fucking not.

In the coaching industry, I come into contact with thousands of women who go through similar phases, which I call *consumption cycles*. They occur when entrepreneurs start doubting themselves and their abilities. They start doubting that they are making the right decisions. They start doubting their intuition. That is when entrepreneurs begin reaching for all the courses and certifications and other things that will give them the answers they think they need. And this consumption cycle happens so easily because they are bombarded 24/7 with marketing aimed at making them doubt themselves.

Now, don't get me wrong: there are times when purchasing a course or a coaching service is exactly what you need, but that is different from looking outside yourself for answers. For example, if you feel good about your decisions, you know your brand and your core values, and you believe your strategy is strong, but you'd like some guidance on how to take yourself to the next level, a coach or course can give you the insight you need. But if you are looking to buy a course in an attempt to "fix yourself" or be successful, that is desperate energy—fearful energy—and you should not be making investment decisions from that place.

It can be a daily battle to trust yourself, to listen to what your gut is screaming for you to do. I get it. But be aware that, when you are constantly consuming, you aren't listening to yourself or taking action in your business. Instead, these cycles lead to exactly what consuming too much food leads to: feeling like you cannot fucking move. You become so full of information that your brain cannot process anything further. It goes into overdrive and doesn't know which thing to move on or sort through first. It is as though your brain is trying to find its way through thick-ass whiteout fog, and the more you consume, the thicker the fog gets. Eventually, the risk is that your brain completely freezes.

When your inaction comes from consuming way too much information, you gotta slow that shit down or cut it off. But to do that, you have to unpack what this is all about—because it's not about the courses. It's about *why* you feel the need to consume all this information. What are you searching for? Could it possibly be that your quest for information comes from a dark secret that lies in the depths of your soul? That maybe this search is more about trying to feed the fear that you aren't enough—not good enough, not smart enough, not thin enough—whatever your weakness is?

I know, it's a kick right in the crotch, and trust me, this wasn't something that came to me overnight. It took a year of fucking failing, ignoring all the warning signs, feeling insecure about myself, feeling insecure in my business, and spending way too much money for me to recognize I was doing all this consuming because I didn't feel good enough as an entrepreneur. Like so many others who sign up with manifestation coaches, business strategists, spiritual coaches, and so on, I thought that the more I consumed and invested, the more likely I would feel that I was enough, that I was whole.

But this void couldn't be filled by *other* people's thoughts/opinions/strategies. I created the void, and I needed to fill it up with *my* thoughts, opinions, and strategy. If you attempt to fill your void with other people's shit, you may ultimately find so much complete and utterly chaotic noise inside your mind that you won't be able to hear yourself anymore. Or you

And just because
you may not "have
your shit together"
the way you believe
your gurus do, and
you have work to do,
doesn't mean you are
any less deserving of
being heard.

won't be able to trust that it is your voice. You will disregard her, ignore her, and abandon her because you will no longer recognize her, when the truth is this: that inner voice is all you need. You are good enough. Yes, maybe you have some work to do. We all do. But there will always be more work. And just because you may not "have your shit together" the way you believe your gurus do, and you have work to do, doesn't mean you are any less deserving of being heard.

I felt a lot of guilt and shame from falling into that consumption cycle. But no personal development journey is perfect, and as human beings, we aren't perfect either—thank God for that. And you know what? My consumption cycle *had* to happen. It really did. Losing myself, and my voice, for a year made me realize two things: (1) I needed to stop searching for the answers outside myself, and (2) I would never allow this shit to happen again.

TAKE F*CKING ACTION
BREAK THE CONSUMPTION CYCLE

Step 1: Stop consuming. It's time to stop buying and get intentional as fuck with what you are going to invest in. Take a few months off from investing in any programs or coaching. (Yes, a coach is telling you to stop investing—for now, anyway.) If you are doing the courses but not implementing the lessons or taking action in your business, you are throwing your cash in a trash can.

Step 2: Figure out what this is really about. Here comes the hard part: ask yourself why you are consuming so much. Where are you not feeling good enough in your life or business? Where is this belief coming from? When was the first time you felt like this? A certification or other course will never make you feel good enough; that is up to you, so ask yourself the tough questions. It's time to start digging and to recognize that you have created this problem and you are the solution to it.

Step 3: Know that you are good enough right now. This step is the most important and sometimes the hardest to take, but you need to start trusting yourself. You need to start listening to your intuition and allow her to guide you back to the right decisions. But for that to happen, you have to recognize that *in this moment you are good enough*. You do not need anything more than what you already have. You do not need to reach another level, another consciousness. You are there, where you need to be, now. Embody this.

TAKEAWAY: You know yourself better than any person on this planet. A coach is there to guide and mentor you, but not to fix you, because you aren't fucking broken. The courses you purchase can be a waste of time and money because they won't make you feel like enough. You have to trust that *you* know what is right for you and your business, you can do this on your own, and you can thrive while doing it.

CHAPTER EIGHT

———

F*CK IT: STAND OUT

My heart is pounding as I stand on the sidewalk in New York City watching all the cars drive by and all the people walking to their destinations at a feverish pace. If you've never been to New York City, let me sum it up by saying this: it is one giant clusterfuck of humans, cars, animals, and energy that sends a vibration through your body like nothing you have ever experienced. The streets are packed full of cars and cabs, no matter what day it is. The sidewalks are filled with pedestrians shoulder to shoulder, pushing through each other, and tourists stopping every three to five seconds to snap a quick selfie near a pizza stand. The streets buzz with excitement and noise.

I am in Midtown, blocks away from the iconic and beautiful Grand Central Terminal. Buildings surround me on every side, buildings so tall that your neck would get cramped even trying to look at the top floors. There is no greenery, no grass, just concrete and pavement lining the blocks. Standing at the corner, I glance down the endless street. Sometimes it seems like the streets go out so far that they never end, that if you kept walking straight, you would end up at the edge of the earth. The

*smell of hot dogs, urine, and exhaust from the cars fills the air,
but I don't care; I am back in my home state and loving every
single second of it.*

*Now I glance at the hundreds of people around me (no fucking joke). The photographer, videographer, and I had snuck off
to a "quiet" street, and yet it is still full of people. I mean, are
there any actual quiet streets in the whole city? Apparently not.*

*"Are you ready?" she asks. "Once the light turns red, we've
got to move." Her face is lit up with excitement, and her energy,
along with her smile, calms me to the bone. She understands
what a big deal this is, and she embraces this idea fully, without
question. My heartbeat quickens, and the pounding becomes so
loud I can hear the echo in my ears. I nod, yes. And then I take
my pants off, right here in the middle of the fucking sidewalk as
people pass by.*

I imagine their thoughts. What the fuck is she doing?
Why is she taking her clothes off? Oy, girl needs to lose a few
pounds. *The thoughts echo in my brain as I slowly fold my pants
and stand there in my boy-short underwear, waiting for the
light to turn red. I can barely breathe, my body trembling, as I
wait for what feels like fucking years and my mind continues to
race.* I can't fucking do this. People are going to laugh at me.
I probably shouldn't have eaten so many bagels this morning.
Ugh! I feel bloated as shit. *But then I hear another interior voice
screaming louder:* BITCH, STOP BLENDING IN, STAND
THE FUCK OUT!

That voice, like a donkey kick right to the crotch, was right.
All those other thoughts screaming inside my head weren't
the voices of those other people; they were my own thoughts
bombarding me. Until now, I had used my body as an excuse,
throughout my entire life, trying to blend in. I had used my
weight as a crutch to not stand out in a crowd or take up space.
To allow myself to play small. I had allowed society's beauty
standards during my youth and adolescent years to dictate

what a "normal" body should look like. And I'd accepted the idea that if I didn't adhere to that standard, I should just spend my life hiding away like some fucking wallflower, never to be seen.

But then, in the middle of an NYC street, I finally had the audacity to be bold as fuck and show my body to the world.

There are three things you need to be to achieve success in the online space and stand out, so grab a pen and take note as we dive into this shit. You need to be

1. Polarizing as fuck, which means to stand in your truth and shout it at the top of your lungs, knowing that people are going to object, disagree, and speak against you. Polarity is the key to building brand loyalty, followers, and exposure, and nothing is more polarizing than a thick-ass girl saying "fuck you" to bullshit beauty standards and baring her ass, rolls and all, on a crowded NYC street knowing people will think she is crazy, ugly, and way too much.

2. Vulnerable, because without vulnerability you have nothing. You need to be especially vulnerable with your audience for them to get to know you. They don't want to know you on a surface level; they want to connect with you on a soul level, and when you open yourself up to being vulnerable, you build trust. Without the trust factor between you and your audience, followers, and clients, you cannot make money. No one will purchase from you if they do not trust you. Granted, learning to be vulnerable is one of the hardest things to do. Baring your soul for the world to rip apart is terrifying, but when it lands with *your* people, it will be the most rewarding experience

of your life. Getting up on that street that day was one of the most vulnerable experiences I had in my life, and the minute we stopped the shoot and I put my clothes back on, I thought I was going to throw up. The entire shoot happened in less than five minutes, but honestly, it felt like I was standing out there forever. Time slowed. But once those pictures were published and I saw them online, I beamed with pride, and my audience lost their shit in the best way possible. I received hundreds of messages and comments about how people loved the photos. It was a thousand percent worth it.

3. Transparent, unlike many of the people online, who only show one aspect of their lives to their followers: the sexy aspect, the aspect that sells. Most people keep everything else that isn't curated for money tight-lipped, but the problem with that is that when the rest of the world experiences so many fucking obstacles with running their businesses, and they don't see their mentors going through the same thing, they feel alone and freakish. When you are transparent, people see that you're not always fearless and that it's OK to be scared shitless and self-conscious. Transparency builds bonds, making people feel less alone in their struggles and insecurities, and it creates connection—and without connection, you don't have shit in your business.

I hadn't planned to strip off my clothes when I first decided to go to New York. I was going to be attending a conference, and when I found out that participants were being gifted a photo shoot from the host, I went into full-fucking-panic mode. I started googling "how to pose for plus-size models" and watched countless hours of YouTube videos, and the night before the photo shoot I didn't sleep a goddamn wink. I was petrified. Then, the next morning as I was lying in bed, I thought, *Wouldn't it be awesome to pose in my underwear with NYC as a backdrop? It would be so on brand . . . with all the chaos and beauty.* I instantly began to feel like I was going to throw up and started talking myself out of it.

But as it turned out, I'd never felt more powerful in my life than at the shoot that day. The adrenaline surging through my veins. The New York City landscape all around me. The chaos, the fucking beauty. It may have taken me thirty-two years to get to that moment of allowing myself to stand out and have the audacity to be bold as fuck, but I was there in that moment of full self-acceptance, and my God was it fucking beautiful.

Likewise, saying "fuck it" to blending into the online space might be the most uncomfortable thing you will ever do. But, my dear, you have to learn how to get comfortable with being uncomfortable. There are times when you are going to have to step way the fuck out of your comfort zone to accomplish things you have always dreamed of. There are times when you are going to have to stretch yourself so far beyond your limits that you fear you will break. There will be times when you will have to do something so bold, so daring, so freakin' brave, that even the thought of it right now in your head makes you want to run and empty your lunch into the porcelain god in your bathroom. Why do we have to do these things? Because when you choose to step out of your comfort zone and stand out, everything changes.

Maybe you are comfortable with where you are in your business right now. Maybe you are sitting on your nice plush couch with your Sherpa blanket and your fleece sweater, comfy as all fuck. It feels good right now, everything so soft and cozy, but being in your comfort zone for too long can kill

When you choose to step out of your comfort zone and stand out, everything changes.

every living fuck out of your business. (Cue "Killing Me Softly with His Song" now!) You have gotten used to a certain way of doing things, but eventually they will provide mediocre results. Do you want better results? Do you want to take your business to the next level? OK then, it's time to stand out—*really* stand out, which might mean burning down the entire comfy room (the metaphorical one; I'm not telling you to set fire to your house). Your comfort zone has become, or will soon become, a danger zone, and unless you get the fuck out of it, and quickly, your business will continue to slowly fizzle out, leaving you feeling unsatisfied with it and possibly in financial ruin. It's time to push yourself again.

Learning how to polarize, expose your vulnerability, and be transparent means getting comfortable with being uncomfortable. Every time you push yourself out of your comfort zone and do something that truly scares the ever-loving piss out of you, you evolve. In fact, you might shift more in that one action than you do in *years* of your life. When you get uncomfortable

- You challenge yourself in a new way, causing quantum shifts in your life and business
- You face a fear that is deeply rooted in your soul, and you make it your bitch
- You give another person permission to do the same

And when that permission is granted, it causes a ripple effect that can be felt through generations of people. When my clients saw the pictures and video of me baring my body in NYC, it gave them permission to do things they were holding themselves back from doing, like the boudoir photo shoot they'd always wanted to do, or standing in their truth with their verbally abusive mother-in-law, or posting videos of themselves pole dancing. When you step out of your comfort zone, it affects not only you, but everyone around you. They see what happens when you reach your potential. They see what they could aspire to be. They create action and step out of *their* comfort zones, starting the cycle over again for everyone who is watching. Isn't that some freakin' magical shit right there?

TAKE F*CKING ACTION
GET UNCOMFORTABLE AF

Step 1: Identify where you are playing small. It's time to look at your business and ask yourself, *Where am I TOO comfortable?* When was the last time you did something that truly scared the piss out of you, that caused your heart to beat so hard in your chest you thought you were going to pass out? Why are you not allowing yourself to grow? Identify when you are spending too much time in that dangerous comfort zone.

Step 2: Get uncomfortable AF. What can you do *right now* in your business that you know would cause massive shifting and change but that makes you want to puke even thinking about it? *DO THAT NOW!* Legit, there is no better time than the present. You have been in that comfy room for too long, and you recognize that being in there is not helping your business. It's time to step out of the room, and it's time to do it now. The more time you waste in that room, the more money you are losing.

Step 3: Get ready to die. Yes, I am being a bit dramatic, but when you have the audacity to be bold and step out of your comfort zone, you will feel like you are going to die. Your body might shake, you may break out in hives, your upper lip may start to sweat even though it has never sweated before. This is because you are facing a fear and growing, and growth sometimes comes with some pain. Know that this is completely freakin' normal. To this day, whenever I do something that makes me uncomfortable, I begin to sweat like a mofo. It's uncontrollable, but it happens. Know that the pain is temporary, and that once you conquer this discomfort, shit is going to take the fuck off.

TAKEAWAY: When you learn how to say "fuck it" and allow yourself to be polarizing, vulnerable, and transparent, your business will stand out. You will enhance your branding, gain more clients, and inspire other women to stand out and reveal their own audacious selves.

CHAPTER NINE

F*CK IT: GO AHEAD AND FAIL

After leaving my job as a pastry chef, I have become a professional dog walker, and I am walking some pups one day in Washington, DC, when I get a call from my husband, Adam.

"Hey, babe. We gotta talk," he says. I know some shit is up right in that moment.

"Is everything OK? The dogs OK?" I panic when I hear the worry in his voice. We've opened up a doggy day care and boarding facility, and he handles that operation during the day when I'm out walking other dogs.

"Ya, everyone is fine," he says. "But a representative from the county just stopped by. Apparently, someone reported that we are running the day care out of our house. We have thirty days to shut it down or we are going to be fined by the county."

I stop dead in my tracks. I have known there was always a possibility of this happening, but I have also been hoping we would find a space to rent before that happened. Honestly, running the day care and boarding out of the house is exhausting, and it has started to drain me physically. Still, I thought I'd have more time. Thirty freakin' days to shut it down? What the hell will I tell my clients? What will I do for money? What about the van we just purchased to drive the dogs back and forth? *Tears well in my eyes, and my throat feels like it is closing in.*

"Babe, you there?" Adam asks.

When I'd walked out of my career as a pastry chef, I was overworked, burned the fuck out, and not sleeping, and I hadn't had more than a day off in over two months. I had no job lined up, no other prospects, nada. All I knew at that moment was that I couldn't take it anymore, and the idea of showing up to work again made me physically ill. But I lived in DC—one of the most expensive cities in the country—and I had bills to pay. I needed to get another job, and quickly, but the idea of returning to the culinary industry made me want to die. I couldn't do it. I had to find an alternative—and fast. Enter Wag!—the dog-walking app.

Wag! pays dog walkers a percentage of the revenues earned for walks or boardings and had just begun to become popular in DC. I thought, *Why not?* I love dogs and I love walking and being outside. Also, I would get to make my own schedule. I quickly started building a massive clientele with the app and was in high demand because I valued people's dogs and went the extra mile to take time with the animals and communicate with their owners. I started getting regular clients, who would then refer me to other people, and soon people were lining up to have me walk their dogs.

I soon started to realize the massive potential of a dog-walking business. If I created my own business, I would get 100 percent of the profits, rather than sharing some of the revenue with Wag! I would *really* be able to dictate my schedule, and my clientele and I could really make something of this. This became my first taste of entrepreneurship. I called my business Puppies & Pastries Dog Care Services, and for two years, I built it from the ground up all by myself. I was the CEO, the employee, and the accountant. I filled all the roles, and by the end of my first year, I'd taken in sixty thousand dollars in cash.

During this time, Adam and I bought a house with a big backyard, fenced it in, and opened a doggy day care facility at our house. We also boarded dogs overnight. That was when Puppies & Pastries income went through the roof. Before I knew it, my little dog-walking business was pulling in around five to eight thousand dollars in cash *a month*. When Adam discovered that, according to county regulations, we were not supposed to be running a doggy day care out of our house, I told him to ignore it. Our neighbors were cool with it. I was making money. And, like, who would find out?

Enter our new neighbors. The house that sits behind our house had been owned by a gentleman who worked night shifts at UPS, and the house had been in his family for generations. When he was relocated and had to sell the house, the new neighbors weren't too keen on us having a doggy day care in our backyard. They were the ones who reported us to the county.

Now, you may be sitting here thinking, *You knew you weren't allowed to do it; what do you expect?* And you are absolutely right. Within thirty days of the county's visit, we shut down the dog day care and boarding services for Puppies & Pastries, and we went from bringing in eight thousand dollars a month to barely two thousand. I felt like a complete failure.

And I was a failure—or so I was repeatedly telling myself. My first attempt at owning my own business had been completely shot out of the sky. My second attempt, in network marketing, was an even bigger failure. My third attempt at my own business, Pastry Chef Fit, was a health coach business I tried to launch at the end of 2018 that focused on healthy desserts. That also fucking flopped. Every single one of my attempts at creating my own business completely failed. Three years of trying so hard to succeed, only to fall flat on my face each time. Three years of failed attempts, frustration, anger, sadness. Even though they were the best things that ever happened to me, they felt like failures because I never reached the level of success I wanted to with each one. I would get one or two steps closer to the stereotypical definitions of success in that specific field and then it would just fail right before I achieved my goal.

But attempt number four, my online coaching business, Fierce as F*ck, blew the fuck up. It was a massive success, and if I hadn't completely tanked on my previous attempts to create my own businesses, I wouldn't have been able to handle the success, obstacles, victories, and shit sandwiches that came with growing a brand from nothing to almost a quarter of a million dollars in less than a year.

Entrepreneurs struggle so hard with a fear of failure. They hold themselves back from achieving greatness, from being their authentic selves, and from launching the best products, products that could change lives, because they are afraid of failing. But the fact of that matter is that you have to say, "Fuck it, I will fail," and have the audacity to do the damn thing anyway. You have to have the audacity to still show the fuck up, to push your hardest, to go all in knowing that you have the chance of completely falling on your face for the world to see. Failing for three years straight is a bash to the ego, a shot to the soul, but it had to happen. I had to learn about audacity and discover that, even though I had failed so many times before, I was going to need to try again. I could not allow multiple failures to control me, to determine my work, my value, or the impact I was going to have on this world.

We all learn to think of failure as a massive monster lurking in the shadows. With its jagged teeth, large body, and long, deadly claws, it is just waiting to pounce on us and rip us to shreds. We are so terrified to awaken the monster that we walk around on eggshells in our businesses, hoping that the crunch

You have to say, "Fuck it, I will fail," and have the audacity to do the damn thing anyway.

won't disturb the beast. This type of mentality keeps us all from achieving the success that we desire.

But you should never need to walk on eggshells in your own business. Your business should be the place for exploration, the place where you are making the greatest amount of noise. It is your place to shine. It is *your* space, so do not allow it to be overtaken by a monster that only exists inside your brain. You have to have audacity. You have to be resilient as fuck when it comes to creating your own business and not allow one failure, or many, to stop you from creating the business you've always dreamed of.

I am going to give it to you straight: there comes a time when you have to recognize that failure is going to happen. There is no way, shape, or form that you will have a successful business without some things going wrong. And those individual failures serve as the bricks that collectively build your pathway to success. Yup, getting corny as shit on you here, but for good reason. There has to be a point in your business, and in your life, when you stop and say, "Fuck it: failure is inevitable." So devour that shit. Know that you will fail. There is no way of stopping it, no way of avoiding it. It *will* happen. Once you accept that—that no matter how perfect you are, no matter how hard you try, no matter what you do, you will fail so fucking hard at some point—you can begin the process of recognizing that failure is the best thing that can happen in your life. Damn, isn't that freeing? Knowing that no matter what you do, you will fall on your face at least once in your business?

There is no success story in this entire world that doesn't have a path of failures laid before it. There is not one single coach, CEO, or leader out there who hasn't failed in their business ventures. Let's take Steve Jobs for example, the former CEO of Apple. Did you know that, ten years after he founded the company, he was fired as the CEO? Apple had felt it was time to shift gears, and Jobs had to walk away from the company he'd created with his blood, sweat, and tears. Apple felt Jobs wasn't innovative enough to carry it into the future. It was marked as one of his biggest failures, but do you know what happened after that? He returned to the company twelve years later and launched it into the stratosphere. What could have been deemed a failure became a triumphant comeback story. He was even once quoted as saying, "I didn't see it then, but it turned out that getting fired from Apple was the best thing that could have ever happened to me." Can you name one CEO who hasn't fallen on their face over and over again? You can't. Every CEO's success story is littered with failure. Every failure leads to lessons, every lesson leads to growth, and every ounce of growth leads to success one way or another. If you aren't failing, you aren't dreaming big enough. It's time to dream big, bitches.

No matter how hard shit looks, feels, or gets: *NEVER GIVE THE FUCK UP*. If you have a dream of becoming successful, you cannot throw in the towel when things get tough and you fail. And let's even break down the concept of never giving up, because I *did* give up on my doggy care business and I *did* give up on my network marketing business. What I mean by never giving up is that, if you know you are meant to be a CEO and you have ventures that never truly felt right and ultimately failed, it's OK to walk away from them. I walked away from those businesses because I *knew* deep in my soul that they were not right for me. Yes, I enjoyed doing them, but I knew they weren't what I was meant to be doing. I could have fought for my doggy day care business: I could have taken out a loan, bought a space, and created a full-fledged brick-and-mortar business. But I didn't want to. Once the initial shock of the business needing to shut down passed, I realized I was relieved that it was closing. I love dogs, but I knew I didn't want to manage a dog care business. I knew that wasn't my true calling. So, instead of fighting for it, I moved on and gave up, because I knew it wasn't my dream.

There are times when you will try something out that you think is what you want, but it doesn't work out. That doesn't mean you should give up your dream. It just means that specific venture wasn't *the right dream*. Sometimes, you can nail it on the first try, find your dream venture, and watch it take the fuck off. Other times, you may have to try on multiple CEO hats to figure out which style is best for you. I had to fail at my dog care business to recognize that a brick-and-mortar-CEO hat wasn't my fit. l had to fail at my network marketing business because that hat felt inauthentic and was made with fake material. It wasn't until I found the right hat—my own brand in the online space—that I knew I had to experience all the wrong things to find that right fit.

And let me address the fact that when you try on different CEO hats and decide one is not the right fit and walk away, it is always the right decision, and you need to trust yourself that it is. Because there will be people who will question your decision. "You are trying another business venture out? Didn't you try network marketing and it didn't work out? Oh, you are starting something new?" They will question your path; they will question your judgment. No matter how many people tell you that it's not worth it, or that you will never succeed, or that you aren't special and should just throw in the towel and return to corporate America: *NEVER GIVE THE FUCK UP.*

TAKE F*CKING ACTION
LEARN FROM FAILURE

Step 1: Figure out your shit. All right, so something didn't work out the way you wanted it to. It's time to reflect (once you recover) and figure out some shit from the situation. What were the things you did wrong? (Yes, we need to own responsibility for this shit.) What were the lessons you learned from this experience?

Step 2: Get the fuck back up. You took a massive hit. You are deep in the trenches, and right now you want to give up. You want to let this situation win, but it's time to move on. Mourn what you need to, release that shit, and stand back up. Be patient with yourself; this can take some time. At first you may only be able to sit up, barely able to use your legs, but you have to try to recover from this. Don't let this one fuckup determine your life. Remember, this is going to lead to something really beautiful one day, but you need to survive this day to see it.

Step 3: Remember the finish line. The biggest thing with failure is to remember that it's part of the process to get you to the finish line: your goals. When shit hits the fan and you feel like you can't get back up, you have to remember that this is a marathon, not a sprint. Reaching your goals takes time, patience, and resilience. It will happen one day, and the only way you *won't* reach them is if you decide to throw in the towel.

TAKEAWAY: I don't necessarily agree with the saying that "nothing worth having comes easy." I believe that some things in life do and *should* come easily, and I would rather say, "Success does not come without resilience." You can't just throw it all the fuck away because you keep running into a brick wall. If your launch fucking flops, get back up and do it again. If your client base has dried up, get out there and launch your services again. Business isn't built solely on success after success. It's built on thousands of failures until one day you fail less often and learn to navigate through those failures with more ease. *Business success is built on resilience.*

CHAPTER TEN

—

F*CK IT: EMBRACE IMPERFECTION

"I don't know what it is," I say to my coach. *"I speak about this shit all the time; I've spoken about these topics a thousand times. But when it comes down to sitting and actually writing a book about them, I just can't."*

Day after day, I open the Google Doc to the book and sit there staring at it, thinking, This is complete shit.

What you are holding in your hands right now, this book, was my literal "fuck it" moment when it came to the battle against perfection.

I had wanted this book to be perfect. It is my first book; it is my heart and soul. My goal was that it would become a global bestseller, but while I was writing it, I fucking suffocated the living shit out of it. And then all that pressure gave me massive writer's block. I created three separate outlines and then trashed all three because they weren't perfect. I would sit down to write a chapter, reread it afterward, edit it—only to decide it still wasn't perfect enough. I eventually decided I needed outside support, and I hired a book coach to help me get the book written, but that sizable investment caused me to put even more pressure on myself to make the book perfect.

As the manuscript barely inched forward, I began to grow ridiculously frustrated, and the writer's block kept on mounting. Ultimately, I saw that, no matter how many times I rewrote a chapter or trashed the outline, and no matter how many eyes I had editing it, my book would never be perfect. And fuck me! Was that a ridiculously hard pill to swallow! This book was—is—all of me. It's a representation of who I am to the core. But then again, if it is a true and accurate representation of me, then it makes sense that it will be anything *but* perfect because I am not perfect by any means. In fact, I take pride in being perfectly imperfect.

I also pride myself on being the person who takes messy, inspired action, who acts first and thinks later. I pride myself on being imperfect in my business. Yet I wasn't allowing myself to be imperfect with this book, repeatedly asking, *Why the fuck am I so hung up on this stupid book? Why can't it just be freakin' good enough?*

And then one day I had a conversation with myself, or as I like to call these introspections, a come-to-Jesus moment. I knew that if I didn't let go of this idea of perfection, I would never get this book done. I knew that if I didn't let it be exactly what it needed to be and instead kept choke-holding it, I would have wasted not only my time, money, and resources but also my coach's. I will never forget that moment of epiphany. Tears welled in my eyes when I finally realized what was needed: I had to have the audacity to follow my own damn advice about putting myself out into the world.

If I didn't allow my book to be imperfect, it couldn't create the impact I desired. In fact, if I didn't stop focusing on perfection, instead of focusing on the person who would ultimately read it, my book would never see the light of day. And that would be a damn shame. No matter what we are selling to this

If I didn't stop focusing on perfection, instead of focusing on the person who would ultimately read it, my book would never see the light of day. And that would be a damn shame.

world, it's not about the person creating it. It's about the person consuming it. That's who needs to hear the message in my book. And that realization is what allowed me to get the book out of the Google Doc and into your hands. Whether you love or hate this book, you have it here to read, and *that* is all that matters.

But after that realization, I had an important next step to take: I had to detach myself from the book to allow it to be perfectly imperfect. What I mean by this is that I was making my book all about *me* and how *I* needed it to be perfect, when in fact the book wasn't for me, it was for *you*. I had to detach my stubbornness about how it had to be presented in a certain way and recognize that the book was going to come out exactly as it was supposed to be so that my message would resonate with the right readers. So that it would resonate with you. Again, I had to let go of this book being about me and let it be for you.

If there is a concept that triggers my soul to the depths of hell, it is the idea that perfection exists, that it is a living, breathing thing, and that if you push yourself hard enough, you will ultimately become perfect. This need to be perfect causes my skin to crawl, my stomach to clench, and my head to ache. It makes me want to flip a fucking Buick in rage. Why does it cause such an adverse reaction in me? Because it is the number-one concept that keeps so many people from showing up as their authentic selves, taking messy, inspired action, and launching their businesses. It keeps them from living the lives they desire, and fucking deserve, all because they are striving to reach this unattainable level of perfection.

Another thing to remember about this need for perfection is that it's not just about not failing. It's actually a need that sets us on the wrong path and, I believe, can be lethal. Yes, lethal. Why? Because striving to be perfect can cause us to do terrible things in the name of perfection. It can cause a young girl to shove her fingers down her throat to rid her body of dinner in an attempt to obtain a perfect body. It can cause a young student to have a mental breakdown during final exams because of the quest for the perfect GPA. It can lead a woman from one glass of wine a day to an entire bottle to cope with the pressure of being the perfect wife and mother. That is why, out of all the concepts we discuss in this book, this inability to let go of perfection is the darkest of the dark, because failing to do so causes harm. It ruins lives. It can destroy you.

And it may seem like I am being a bit melodramatic, but this is not just a problem on the personal level. I have seen countless entrepreneurs fall to this need for perfection, and their businesses never take off. Or products don't get launched. Or too much money is spent on courses or too much time is spent obsessing over graphics or websites. All this in search of perfection, and meanwhile, these entrepreneurs completely neglect their audiences. Moreover, this drive for perfection causes these business owners to get stuck in the hamster wheel of perfection paralysis, and before they even see what's coming, their businesses completely tank.

I mean, how could they succeed in those circumstances? This happens when entrepreneurs set impossible standards, become overwhelmed as fuck, and then completely freeze. Sometimes they even start acting like complete assholes when they can't achieve the results they want. And then they stop showing up altogether. Sound familiar? I am sure it does. Every single person on this planet has gone through this cycle at least once in their lifetime, whether professionally or personally—and if they are lucky, it happens only once. But typically this cycle is on repeat all their lives and they can never truly break free.

The odd thing I wonder about is this: *Who really wants to be perfect anyway?* Never failing, never making mistakes, never experiencing cringeworthy moments? My goodness, does that sound like a boring-as-fuck life to me! Don't you agree? If you aren't experiencing imperfection, then are you even truly living? Probably not. You are probably just going through the motions of life, too scared to be anything less than perfect and presenting a facade. You smile even when you want to cry. You swallow your anger although it burns your throat on the way down. You have to fake everything. And that isn't something to strive for; in fact, it's just plain sad. It's a life without feelings, without fire, without pain. And that is no life.

Perfection is an endless race that you can never win. Each time you strive for the finish line—running and running on the racecourse, your body pouring sweat, your bones aching, your lungs hot and stinging—you ultimately discover you can't find the line of perfection because it never existed to begin with. Being imperfect can feel like the opposite of running an impossible marathon because it gives you room to breathe. It gives you the space to fuck up royally and *still be OK afterward.* I cannot stress that enough. When you embrace imperfection, you are able to feel your emotions at a cellular level—all of them, so intense and yet so beautiful. Imperfection can actually be the most gorgeous thing on this planet. Strive to be perfectly imperfect.

TAKE F*CKING ACTION
STEP OUT OF PERFECTION

Step 1: Identify where this bullshit comes from. Where did you first feel the need to be perfect? Was it a concept *you* came up with? Was it something that was pushed onto you by a parent, society, teachers? When you identify where this need came from, it's easier to recognize that it wasn't you who put this on yourself. It was other people's bullshit, their beliefs, that were cast on you because of *their* inadequacies. Remember, they grew up in the same cycle you did, also always striving for a perfection they never achieved. Who knows? Maybe that made them bitter as all hell and they're turning that bitterness toward you. Either way, it's not *you*.

Step 2: Release this bullshit. It's time to release this fear of imperfection. Rather than focusing on the idea that everything needs to be perfect, how can you empower the idea of imperfection in your head? In the minds of others? You empower other people to be imperfect by showing them that you are fucking human and you make mistakes. By showing them you are on the same level as them, that you have flaws, you will actually connect more deeply with them and give them permission to show up in this world as themselves.

Step 3: Practice patience. Y'all need to recognize that letting go of perfection isn't a process where you just snap your fingers and—*poof!*—magically heal everything overnight. This is something that will take a bit of practice and patience. You will have times when you crush embracing your imperfections, and it will feel like you are on top of the world. You will also have times when you get stuck right back up in the hamster wheel of perfection and waste countless hours of your life moving absolutely nowhere. You need to give yourself some freakin' grace and allow yourself to fuck up *a lot* during this deconditioning process. It will take time. Keep on keeping on.

TAKEAWAY: You can choose right now to continue on your path toward perfection, but I will tell you: this need will destroy your soul. Maybe not today, maybe not tomorrow, but one day you will wake up and realize it has all been a big fat lie, and on that day, my heart will break for you. Or you can choose to embrace a new need to be sloppy, to fuck up, to fail so hard you don't know whether you will be able to get back up. Embrace a need to have freedom and space to play. A need to be imperfect, the only need worth striving for.

CHAPTER ELEVEN

F*CK IT: EAT THE SHIT SANDWICH

"Be safe, NOLA residents, as you evacuate the city." I stare at the tweet on my phone. Da fuck? Why would New Orleans residents have to evacuate the city?

The tweet came from a pastry chef I interned with when I lived in New Orleans, so I know it's legit, but I haven't heard anything on the news about an evacuation. What the hell is going on?

I immediately jump up from the couch in my living room and run into my office to open my laptop. I quickly search Google, typing in "New Orleans evacuations," and become bombarded with news articles.

"New Orleans Residents Start to Evacuate as Hurricane Ida Makes Her Way to Shore."

"Category 4 Hurricane Ida to Make Landfall in New Orleans in Two Days."

"Will the Levies Hold? Will Hurricane Ida Be as Catastrophic as Hurricane Katrina?"

"Hurricane Ida to Make Landfall on Anniversary of Katrina."

I feel like I'm dying inside. I'd had no idea that a hurricane had even been discovered, let alone that it was heading for New Orleans. "What the fuck am I going to do?" *I yell out loud.*

"What's wrong?" *Adam says from his office, adjacent to mine.*

"There is a fucking hurricane that is supposed to make landfall in New Orleans in two fucking days!" *I yell.*

"Oh fuck!" *He comes into my office.* "What are you going to do?"

You see, I was scheduled to host two in-person retreats in New Orleans, four days after Ida was now expected to make landfall. Yup, complete shit show. I was supposed to have a dozen women flying from all over the country to come stay with me in New Orleans to learn all about Human Design and their businesses, and here we were, less than a week out, and a damn hurricane was about to ruin everything. I immediately went into crisis mode and messaged my team to let them know what was going on.

"I am not going to cancel anything until I see it make landfall," I typed. "We will assess the damage and then make the decision on what to do."

To say I was glued to my TV for the next three days would be an absolute understatement. I was receiving updates from the Weather Channel nonstop. I was watching live footage of the French Quarter, trying to assess the damage. I was on my laptop every five minutes, refreshing the screen to get the latest update. Thank God, the levies held in New Orleans, but the city ended up taking a good deal of damage. As I watched the way people there were hurting and suffering, and saw the damage on the news, I knew that the entire city needed time and space to heal. Which meant I knew I had to call it. We needed to respect the city, and so we pushed our event out into the future. I wasn't about to risk the lives not only of the women flying in but also of the residents of New Orleans who were trying to heal in the aftermath.

I love New Orleans; in fact, I had lived there for a few months while interning at Domenica, a local restaurant. I have visited seven-plus times, and the city means everything to me. It broke my heart to know they were experiencing another massive hurricane that caused so much damage. When we did eventually host the retreat in January 2022, the city was still recovering from the damage, with blue tarps remaining on rooftops. Months later, the city continued hurting.

My team and I scrambled to adapt. We had to communicate with all the vendors (most of whom did not have cell service or power), and I went back and forth for days with the rental agency that had found our venue and was trying to make us honor the date even though the house didn't have power. In fact, it was so extensively damaged that we had to find another house when we rescheduled our event the next year. I cried so much during this time, out of hurt, out of sadness—both for the city of New Orleans enduring this tragedy and for myself, as this wasn't the first time a major obstacle had gotten in my way.

Hurricane Ida hit in 2021, but I'd also had to cancel two in-person retreats the previous year when COVID-19 hit and the entire country went into lockdown. Like everyone, I spent weeks trying to adjust to this new normal of being stuck in the house all day every day, on top of working to reschedule the retreat venue that had already been fully paid for. It was a nightmare, and not only for my business; people were suffering globally. Grocery stores couldn't keep up with demand, people were getting sick and dying by the thousands, everyone was locked in their houses not knowing whether the pandemic would last a few days, weeks, or months. I had no idea what was going to happen the next day, let alone when I could reschedule my retreats. Months were filled with panic, uncertainty, and having to adapt at a moment's notice due to the growing urgency of the pandemic.

So, you could say I became used to eating shit sandwiches in my business during the pandemic, but when another one came with the hurricane? Lordy, that hit me right in the gut, and honestly it took me an entire month to bounce back from that. I felt the full spectrum of emotions during that month. I was mentally, physically, and emotionally exhausted. But when times get tough in your business and you are dealing with shit sandwiches, you sometimes have to say, "Fuck it. Give me the shit sandwiches—I will eat them all." You must have the audacity to be adaptable to any situation, any shit sandwich the Universe sends you.

With every uplevel comes great responsibility. Yes, I'm harnessing my inner Yoda voice when I say this, but it's true. An uplevel is a moment when something absolutely fucking spectacular happens, a moment when you and your business evolve to the next level. It's a term that you hear over and over again in the coaching world. With every uplevel, you will reach a new degree of income, you will evolve and grow, and your business will change. But what a lot of people don't tell you is that with all that beauty comes a fuck ton of shit sandwiches.

Definition of *shit sandwich*: an event or obstacle that occurs in your life that shakes the very ground you walk on. That causes you to fall so hard, you eat shit. Please hold the mayo.

You cannot have the good without also sometimes having the absolutely fucking terrible. That's why it's a sandwich: because shit often happens in the midst of otherwise good things. These obstacles also come when you least expect them and always at the wrong damn time for your business. Now, don't get me wrong: something bad isn't going to happen every time your business reaches a new level, but what a lot of entrepreneurs fail to tell you is that most of their businesses' uplevels occur after being hit with massive shit sandwiches. Everything seems fine and dandy and then—*BAM!*—shit sandwich right to the kisser.

But shit sandwiches aren't all that bad, because you often also discover a few things about yourself when you are chowing down on one:

- How resilient you are
- How brave you are
- That you can handle more than you give yourself credit for
- How smart you are
- How quick on your feet you are
- How fucking incredible you are at adapting to any stone thrown in your path

You learn more about yourself when dealing with a shit sandwich than you ever do when life is easy peasy lemon squeezy. For some reason, you need to go through this obstacle to learn a valuable lesson you will take with you for the rest of your life. A lesson that will change who you are to your core. Lessons aren't always made from positive situations; they are often made from terrible mistakes or unfortunate events beyond your control. Without those shit-sandwich lessons, you wouldn't be the person you are today, and you wouldn't become the person you are yet to become.

Eating these shit sandwiches was the best thing that could have happened to me. I know, shocker, but it's true. Because of them, I was able to realize how quick I can be on my feet and how fast I can adapt to any situation. They made me realize how strong my team was and how well they supported me in my business. And when I did finally get my first in-person

Lessons aren't always made from positive situations; they are often made from terrible mistakes or unfortunate events beyond your control.

events, it made me appreciate everything about those so much more. Yes, they represent trying experiences, but what comes afterward is so much better. I think of the saying "The grass is greener on the other side" whenever it comes to shit sandwiches. Once you get through the difficulty, the grass will be greener wherever you are. In fact, shit sandwiches define who we are in our businesses and as leaders.

I was devastated to postpone the events, but in reality, it worked out for the best: we were able to get into my favorite champagne bar, which had been scheduled to be closed for the original date. I was able to bring the women to Pat O'Brien's, a famous piano bar, which reopened right before we arrived. We ended up getting *two* massive houses to replace the one we originally booked, which gave us so much more space. And the people of New Orleans welcomed us with open arms. All these beautiful experiences happened because of a shit sandwich. It all happened for a reason.

TAKE F*CKING ACTION
DEVOUR THOSE SHIT SANDWICHES

Step 1: Recognize the lesson. You are going through this for a reason; there is a lesson to all this madness. When shit sandwiches are being thrown at you left and right, ask yourself, *What do I need to learn from this? Where do I need to grow? What do I need to release? Where do I need to shift?* Get really clear on *why* this is happening, because the Universe does everything for a reason. The hurricane had to upend our event to teach my team and me how to shift plans and adapt to a changing situation. It brought us together as a team when we had to reach out to vendors, change the house location, and communicate with the people who were coming to the retreat.

Step 2: Stay the course. Shit sandwiches can range in duration; they can occur as one specific event or they can last for months or—in my case—years. While eating shit sandwiches, you tend to get really down on yourself, and my biggest piece of advice for alleviating this is to remember that your situation is only temporary. It may feel like it is taking forever to get through, but you *WILL* get through it. One day, the fog will dissipate and there will be nothing but clear skies. Keep on pushing. And right now, you may be saying, "That's trash, Amanda. I won't ever get through this." But you will because there is literally no other option. You *HAVE* to get through it.

Step 3: Learn to laugh. Yes, you need to learn to laugh at these situations when they come up. And no, I don't mean laugh at the fact that a hurricane or a pandemic happened—those are extremely tragic. What I mean is that if you don't laugh at the adaptation itself, you will go insane. These are trying times, and you need to have a bit of a sense of humor to survive them. Laugh about how ridiculous the situation is, laugh about how you are scrambling about. Laugh about how it's out of your control. Laugh about it—you just have to.

Step 4: Remember that adaptation is evolution. Recognize that every single time you are forced to adapt in a situation, you grow: emotionally, mentally, physically. These events test you, but when you come out on the other side, you will have evolved in a tremendous way. You will be wiser, more creative, and more resilient, and all these beautiful things will have grown out of this shit show.

TAKEAWAY: Business is a roller coaster, and you've got to be able to sit through the ride. It will have ups and downs and twists and turns, and will sometimes leave you vomiting in a trash can. But the reason roller coasters are so thrilling is because of that uncertainty: not knowing when the drops will happen or when the next turn will come up. You have to adapt to the situation, take a deep breath, and prepare yourself for the ride.

CHAPTER TWELVE

F*CK IT: BELIEVE IN MAGIC

"What color house do you want?" I ask.

"Blue!" my nephew yells.

"Or maybe white," my niece chimes in.

"What color is the front door?"

"Yellow!" They both scream as they start to understand what is happening.

"How many bedrooms?"

"Five! That way everyone can have their own rooms," my nephew says.

"Well, Mikey and Danny can share a room," my niece says. "But yes, five, so we can have a playroom!"

Children are magical. I am blessed to have seven nieces and nephews in my life. My sister has three daughters, and my brother has three sons and a daughter. I find all the children absolutely fascinating. There is something about them that is so pure, so beautiful: they still believe in all their hearts and souls that magic exists.

It has become a tradition with my brother's children that they each get to come up and spend a week with me during the summer. They live in North Carolina, and I wish we could get together more often than holidays and these summer visits, but we work with what we've got.

I will never forget what happened one summer. My oldest niece and nephew, who were around nine and ten at the time, were extremely interested in my spirituality work. Let me preface this by saying, although I dabble here and there in the woo-woo, I am definitely *not* a spirituality coach, and I am not as fully immersed in it as some others are. But I do some daily practices to help center myself, and my office usually contains crystals, chakra stones, intention candles, sage, palo santo, chakra clear spray, and oracle cards—all lined up on my shelves, and all of which seem very magical to children. The kids kept asking me questions about which crystal did what, why I pulled oracle cards, and what the cards meant. They even asked if they could help me clear the energy from the room. It was freakin' adorable, and I wanted to harness that interest. I wanted them to know that my house was a safe space to ask questions, be curious, and believe in magic.

One of my lifelong dreams has been to buy a house for my brother, his wife, and their kids. They live in a small house, and it's a bit cramped. Their children love and adore the house, but my dream is for them to have their own rooms, their own space, in a massive house that they can run through screaming at the top of their lungs, with a yard they can play and run in. A place where they can create memories that will last a lifetime, so that no matter how tough shit might get, they could always return to a safe place they call home. A space where they can always just look back at their lives and think, *I was safe, secure, taken care of.* I've wanted them to be happy, and they were not happy in their current living conditions. They loved their house, but I wanted them to have more.

When the kids started expressing interest in some of my spiritual stuff, I wanted to include them in my vision. I wanted them to feel like they were a part of it because ultimately this visit was never about me; it was about them. So one day, while sitting in my office, I had an idea. Let's make them a part of a manifestation process. Let's show them what that's all about. I called the two oldest into my office and told them we were going to do a manifestation exercise. I explained to them a bit about manifestation and that it basically means bringing dreams into reality by speaking them into existence. They grabbed all my intention candles (success, money, abundance, gratitude) and lit every single one of them. They saged the room to clear the energy. They were laughing and smiling as I grabbed my giant-ass easel from the corner. I told them each to sit down because we were going to create their dream house. I explained to them that nothing was off limits; they could have whatever they wanted in their house. A pool? It's yours! A fenced-in backyard for the dogs? Done! Their faces glowed with excitement as I grabbed my Sharpie from the jar and said "Go!"

But then a look of intense confusion shadowed their faces. I told them, "I want you to imagine your dream house. I want you to tell me everything you want in it. I want your imaginations to go crazy." Recognizing they needed a little nudge, I started asking questions:

"How many bathrooms do you want?"

"Three bathrooms, and two of them have to have double sinks."

The more questions I asked, the more excited they grew. "I want a pool, but with a fence so the dogs don't jump into it and rip the liner. A fenced-in backyard so our dogs can run around. A back porch that's screened in just like the one you have, Aunt Mandy. A firepit. And I want Grandma to have her own apartment above the garage, so she is always around."

Holy shit, man, did this start to choke me up. I could feel myself becoming emotional as I watched them get more and more into this exercise, experiencing true limitlessness, true imagination. It was incredible to watch two children be able to express their wants and desires in a safe space—where they weren't going to be shut down or told *no* or admonished because what they wanted wasn't realistic. We kept going and going until every freakin' inch of that easel paper was covered. Afterward, they asked if they could hold the candles and get a picture with the board, and it was the most beautiful moment. And then what happened next was just pure fucking magic.

I told the kids that, for this manifestation to come true, we had to open the windows and blow out the candles, like a birthday wish. This way, the smoke would make it up to God/ Universe so our wants and needs could be heard. We opened the windows, and the kids blew out the candles. They waved the smoke out the windows with their hands, sending it to the heavens to be received, but one candle refused to stop smoking: the *success* candle. In fact, that damn candle smoked for twenty minutes. I had lit that candle at least a dozen times before, and every time I blew it out, the smoke would disappear. But now, this time, the kids and I stood there in complete amazement as the excitement on their faces brightened even more.

"Aunt Mandy!! This means that it's 95 percent going to come true!" my nephew said, a twinkle in his eyes. Pure. Fucking. Magic. It wasn't until after this beautiful experience was over that I had a complete "holy shit" moment.

While we were going through the manifestation exercise— when the kids' imaginations were going wild—they never qualified their dreams based on what they deemed to be realistic. But when you ask adults to speak their dreams aloud, and *if* you can actually get them to say anything, it is usually followed by qualifications and disclaimers.

"But it's too much."

"I want it, but I don't really need it."

"I would love this, but it's unrealistic at this time."

"There is no logical way this can happen."

"I don't have the resources to get there."

"I shouldn't want this. I should pick something more practical."

And the list goes on and on. Many adults cannot dream without automatically shutting that dream down a millisecond later. Don't even get me started on the amount of guilt and shame that is attached to actually declaring your wants and desires out loud. We are so conditioned to repress our hopes that we can't even fathom the idea that something magical might actually happen. It's as if the day we found out Santa was really our parents we lost all faith in the impossible happening.

Adults get so used to being told *no*—something is unrealistic, or they should just be grateful—that they form this automatic self-defense mechanism, where the second they have a dream, they shut themselves down. Putting yourself out there by expressing your hopes and dreams is an extremely vulnerable process, and when it is met with resistance, limiting beliefs, and sometimes just dickhead comments, you feel betrayed. You feel like you are standing naked on a stage, and everyone is pointing and laughing at you. When this happens, you stuff your dreams into an empty box and bury them deep down inside, never to be accessed again.

With a child, there is so much lightness in dreaming, so much potential. As I stood there watching my niece and nephew dream their wildest, lightest dreams, my mind was blown. Imagine if you could harness this magical power as an adult. Imagine if you could tap into all that limitless potential without the emotional torment that follows. My niece and nephew were given the ability to dream that day, the *permission* to dream. Even if the dream doesn't come true exactly as described, the experience showed them the possibilities of what can happen when you dream big.

What if you gave yourself the permission to believe again?

Likewise, imagine the fucking power of manifestation and what it could do to your life. Manifestation is magic; it *is* Santa Claus. Don't get me wrong: I used to disregard manifestation as just another hot-button term in the personal development industry. But it holds so much validity, and I had to give it a chance and *actually* try manifesting to see it come to fruition. I had to believe in all my heart and soul that whatever I truly desired could be brought into my life. I started small, trying to manifest a few dollars here and there, and before I knew it, the Universe was sending me the money I desired. The evidence was provided, and I became hooked, but first I had to *believe* that it truly could happen.

If you don't believe it works, it's not going to work. If you don't believe in this magic, it's never going to come to fruition. If you can't say your dream out loud and believe in it, see it, and visualize the possibilities ahead of you, it will never happen. I know that sounds harsh; it is a realization I had to come to myself—and it was not an easy one. You need to speak the words out loud without all the bullshit tied to them. Your words need to be as light as a balloon so they can float up to the Universe, so she can hear them and help you by capturing them and placing them firmly into your reality. If every time your light words are followed by that *I shouldn't want this* or *I'm not worthy of this* or *I should just be grateful* bullshit, then it would be like tying a ten-ton brick onto the end of the balloon. It will sink right back to the ground. But if your balloon is like a child's, it will fucking fly. It will be beautiful. It will be light. It will be something beyond this world: magical.

What if, instead of negating everything, you just allowed yourself to believe that anything can happen? What if you allowed yourself to desire, without tying your worthiness to it? What if you gave yourself the permission to believe again? To recognize that you are good enough, worthy enough, smart enough? To see that if the desire wasn't worth having, you wouldn't be having it? All this is possible, but only if you allow it to be, because you are the only one who can. No one else. Yes, people can chime in and push our dreams to the ground, but we allow that to happen. You have the ability to stand up for your dreams. You can speak the words to tell people to shut their dammmmnnn mouths, and if you don't, that's on you. You stand in your own way when it comes to achieving those dreams, because if *you* can't even believe in them, how do you expect others to?

TAKE F*CKING ACTION
ADD SOME FUCKING MAGIC BACK

Step 1: Step into the dream room. It's time to blow up the motherfucking picture of what you want your business to be. When was the last time you allowed yourself to get really creative and dream about your end goals for your business? I want you to let your imagination go wild—nothing is off limits, truly. You may even want to try to *expand* the dream. Want to write a book? Great, but blow that dream up even bigger: What if it was a national bestseller? What if it led you to speaking gigs all over the country? What if your book's success landed you on Oprah's Book Club List? Expand the living shit out of your dreams.

Step 2: Don't be the critic. Logic is bullshit, and it's time to throw logic out the window. When you are in the dream room, you are not allowed to negate any of your dreams. You are not allowed to say, "It's not logical to make this much this year when I made that much last year," or "I can't sell ten seats to my program if I can't sell one." Do not allow yourself to get caught up in logic and expectations in the dream room. This is where you get to be bold, wild, and crazy with your dreams without the inner critic speaking up.

Step 3: Beware of your inner asshole. With your inner critic comes your inner asshole, or as one of my clients called it, your inner mean girl. When you allow yourself to dream, this spawn-of-Satan demon child comes out and says shit like "You aren't good enough," or "You will never accomplish this," or "You aren't expert enough for this," and so on. It's time to shut this Regina George of a bitch up. In the dream room, you are the best version of yourself, and that person doesn't take negative talk, limiting beliefs, or any of that shit from anyone. If you start to see these inner mean-girl sayings bubbling up, write them down on a piece of paper. When you are done in the dream room, look at that piece of paper and tell yourself all the reasons you *are* good enough, expert enough, smart enough, etc. After you do that, burn those bitches up. Release them into the earth or sky, and tell your inner asshole to sit down and shut the fuck up. This is your time.

TAKEAWAY: Allow yourself to connect to your inner child, to take their hand, to step into their dream room. Allow yourself to dream so big that it takes up all the space around you. Allow the vast possibilities to stream from your body and paint the most beautiful picture in front of you. Allow your dreams to push the walls out around you, to lift you higher and higher into the sky. Allow yourself to dream so big that it scares the living shit out of everyone around you and inspires others to torch their limitations and dream again, too. Allow yourself to experience that pure magic; it's the most powerful thing in this world, so you might as well use it.

CHAPTER THIRTEEN

ONE LAST AUDACIOUS THOUGHT: BURN IT TO THE F*CKING GROUND

"Do you even want to do dessert videos anymore?" my coach asks me.

I stare at her blankly through the computer screen. "What do you mean? Of course I do."

"It doesn't seem like you do. You are coming up with all these reasons why you shouldn't do it. Honestly, it doesn't seem like it's something you actually want *to do."*

"No, I do," I respond defensively.

"But do *you?" she replies quickly.*

I don't.

We have reached the end of our path together, and I want to part with some final words for you. If your business does not bring you joy and happiness—if it doesn't make you want to pee yourself—then there is something I need you to do for me:

BURN IT TO THE FUCKING GROUND.

If your business does not bring you joy and happiness—if it doesn't make you want to pee yourself—then there is something I need you to do for me: burn it to the fucking ground.

It was December 2018, and I had spent the past year bouncing from a network marketing company to my first attempt at creating an online brand. Since I had a background as a pastry chef and was a fitness enthusiast with experience coaching clients through weight loss, I believed it would be a natural transition to become a health and wellness coach specializing in teaching women how to make healthy versions of their favorite foods and desserts. I created the brand Pastry Chef Fit. I had already launched a dessert course and a cookbook for the brand, but they had tanked, so my coach and I jumped on a call to try to strategize my next move.

Desserts and weight loss coaching had initially seemed like a natural fit for me, given my background with more than six years in the culinary industry, my experience in weight loss coaching through Jenny Craig when I was in my twenties, and my network marketing company (not to mention my teenage Dexatrim habit). My social media followers were also used to me talking about all things food and fitness. It should have been easy, and at first I believed I was going to make a killing. But as I dove into creating the brand and marketing my services, everything started to feel off. I was doing whatever my coach told me to do, and yet nothing was working. I had created the website, created the offers, made sales pages, spent money on Facebook ads, and was trying to launch it all—but I still had nothing to show for it. I had known deep in my soul that I didn't want to do health and wellness coaching, but I figured it would be stupid for me *not* to do it given my experience.

When my coach started asking what I really wanted to do, I mentioned a new idea. "I don't know, I was thinking of switching to life coaching. I had an idea for a course."

She reminded me that I'd already switched from doggy day care to network marketing to my new culinary brand. She also reminded me that I'd put so many hours into what I'd already created and suggested that maybe we just needed to rework some structures to make it more enjoyable. She wasn't telling me no; she wasn't saying that I couldn't succeed at life coaching. She was just trying to help. But for some reason, by herding me in the direction of continuing to market my health and wellness brand, she triggered an inner voice. *OHHHHH HELLLLL NOOOO!*

"You're right. Maybe I just need a few days off," I said. But then I got off the call almost immediately and formulated a plan to abandon Pastry Chef Fit and create a new life coaching brand. I knew that it meant walking away from months of building a brand, working on websites and sales pages, and creating courses. All that work was going to go down the drain, but I knew, deep in my soul, that it was the right decision to make. Pastry Chef Fit wasn't my passion, and every single time I worked on anything for that brand, it felt like the energy was being sucked out of my body. Every hour of recording the videos, of editing, of marketing—all of it felt wrong. I had to come to terms with the fact that I never really wanted that brand, and it was time to let it go.

So yes, you heard me! Burn your business to the ground if you've lost (or never had) your passion for it. Here is your permission slip. You've heard about all the things I did to try to get to a point where I was in love with a business that made my heart sing. And you've read about all the things I fucked up along the way. None of what I have today would have happened if I hadn't said "fuck it" each time and burned those ideas to the ground. Some of them were great. Some of them sucked. None of them were going to get me to where I wanted to be, so I grabbed the matches.

After reading this book, I hope you recognize that *you* are the only one who knows your business at a soul level. *You* are the only one who can make the right decisions. *You* are the only person with the right answers, the only one who can be trusted to lead you down the right path. If your business does not turn you on so badly that you need to squeeze your thighs together to keep from exploding, it does not belong in your life.

I know what you're thinking: *I just read an entire freakin' business book and now this bitch is telling me to burn my business to the ground?* Ummmmm, *YUP*. Hear me out. If your business is causing you so much grief and so much angst, you will never be a successful CEO. I don't mean to be harsh, but your energy is everything in your business, and if your energy isn't 1,000 percent committed to your business and the success of it, you will eventually self-sabotage. Or you will succumb to fear. Or you will feel as if you are trudging through mud for years. Who the fuck wants that? Absolutely no one.

You wanted to create this business to bring you happiness, and right now, it's not doing that. The most powerful thing you can do when something isn't working for you is to let it go. Be that bitch from *Frozen* and cast your business aside. It has done all that it can for you at this point. You have grown, you have evolved, you have discovered yourself, and now it's time your business does the same. Don't worry, you aren't "starting over." It's not like all your hard work is going to—*poof!*—disappear. You will take the lessons you have learned, the shit sandwiches you have eaten, and the knowledge and wisdom you have gained, and you will *create* something *BETTER*.

If I hadn't started fires along the way, I'd never have created Fierce as F*ck, a brand that brings me so much joy and passion and has created such an impact on hundreds of women's lives. Allowing yourself the permission to burn it to the ground will give you the freedom to create a business that makes you so happy you cannot wait to wake up in the morning and work on it. You will create a business that is in 100 percent alignment with your values, beliefs, desires. You will create a business where *YOU* call the fucking shots and don't let anyone tell you otherwise. You will build a business that will keep you orgasmically satisfied for the rest of your life. Isn't that something worth exploring?

So please take what you have learned from this book with you during your reconstruction period. If certain chapters didn't resonate with you—if they didn't "slap," as the kids say—then say, "FUCK IT!" and don't use them. Yes, you heard that right. If my advice didn't help or doesn't align with you, say, "FUCK IT!" Figure out what *does* work for you and implement the living shit out of it. There are no wrong answers in business. There are undiscovered ones, and paths less traveled, but there is nothing *wrong* in business. Business is personal and individualized, so have the audacity to allow it to be *100 PERCENT THAT BITCH.*

ABOUT THE AUTHOR

Amanda King is an empowerment coach who helps entrepreneurs build authentic businesses. In just three years she was able to grow the value of her brand, Fierce as F*ck, to over half a million dollars using organic marketing techniques. After spending a decade working in corporate America as a pastry chef, she left it all behind to build her unique brand of "blue-collar coaching," a strong antidote to the glossy #bossbabe entrepreneurship that's peddled online ad nauseam. She focuses on leading with integrity, vulnerability, transparency, and, most importantly, authenticity. She strives to help every entrepreneur find their voice, be bold, and take up as much space as humanly possible in this world.

King currently resides in Virginia with her three dogs and enjoys spending time with her many (seriously, there are a lot of them) nephews and nieces.

CPSIA information can be obtained
at www.ICGtesting.com
Printed in the USA
JSHW032308121122
33018JS00004B/5